Computer Security Quiz Book

A Compendium of over 1,700
short questions with answers

S.R. Subramanya

Exskillence

San Diego, USA

Table of Contents

Preface

Computer security has become one of the areas of Computer Science which has attracted considerable attention both in terms of research efforts in foundational mathematical and computational techniques, as well as development of policies, products, and services. It has spawned several new subareas which were non-existent just a few years ago. Its importance and relevance has been growing phenomenally, thanks in large part to computers becoming the enablers of almost all aspects of the contemporary society – manufacturing, engineering, utilities, transportation, automotive, retail, commerce, finance, healthcare, etc. This necessitates computer security to be built into the design of several diverse hardware and software systems, based on a variety of policies, using a wide range of techniques and tools, and catering to a wide variety of applications in different domains. The other important factors contributing to the dire necessity of computer security are the phenomenal increases in the number and diverse types of devices that are being increasingly interconnected via various kinds of networks, and the apparent non–existence of guaranteed schemes of securing networked computing systems against attacks.

Computer security is an important course in Computer Science curricula with real-world relevancy. There are even degree programs in Computer Security, and a variety of certification courses. Basic knowledge of the fundamental principles and techniques of the various facets of computer security is absolutely necessary for computer security professions. Also, it is important and beneficial for professionals in other areas of computing/IT as well as other related/ relevant areas to have some peripheral knowledge of contemporary issues in computer/information security, since the overall security of systems is dependent on informed users in addition to good technologies.

For students who are taking a first course on Computer Security, or have already taken the course, or have otherwise learnt the topics of the course, there are not many comprehensive resources for a quick assessment/testing of the fundamental understanding of the principles, concepts, and techniques of the many aspects of Computer Security. This book aims to fill that need. This is a quick assessment book / quiz book with over 1,700 short questions with answers. It covers all the major topics in a typical first course in Computer Security – Cryptography, Authentication and Key Management, Software and Operating Systems Security, Malware, Attacks, Network Security, and Web Security.

Unique features of this book.

- Over 1,700 short questions, with answers.
- Questions are of only two types – True/False and sentence completion.
- All questions are single sentence and have consistent format.
- Questions have a wide range of difficulty levels.
- Questions are designed to test a thorough understanding of the topical material.
- Questions also cover popular ones asked in internship / job interviews.

Who could benefit from this book?

- Students who are currently taking a first course in Computer Security could use this book for self–assessment and to focus on topics one is unsure about. This helps in improving the performance in tests and exams.
- Students who have already finished a first course in Computer Security, and are preparing to take written exams and/or interviews for industry/companies.
- Persons preparing for certification (ex. CISSP) exams.
- Faculty can use it as a resource to quickly select a few questions as part of a quiz being prepared.
- Professionals trying to make a switch to Computer/Information security industry could use it as a source of self–assessment.

- Interviewers / Managers / Technical leads could use it to make a quick assessment of the candidates' fundamental understanding of computer security principles, in phone / personal interviews.
- Participants and quiz masters in quiz competitions may draw upon the vast pool of questions/answers.

Notes

- The questions in each topical section are not necessarily in any particular order.
- Occasionally (although rarely) a question is phrased in multiple ways.
- Multiple-choice questions (MCQs) have not been used on purpose.
- Questions cover topics of fundamental nature which are common to all modern / contemporary security systems.
- 'Hash code' and 'message digest' are used synonymously.
- Network related questions are used in the context of TCP/IP protocol stack.
- Features specific to any commercial security system/product are not used in the questions.

Acronyms used in the book have been expanded in their first use/reference. They are given below for convenience.

ACL – Access Control List
AES – Advanced Encryption Standard
AH – Authentication Header
ARP – Address Resolution Protocol
CA – Certificate Authority
CBC – Cipher Block Chaining
CFB – Cipher Feed Back
DDoS – Distributed Denial of Service
DES – Data Encryption Standard
DHCP – Dynamic Host Configuration Protocol
DNS – Domain Name Service
DoS – Denial of Service
DSS – Digital Signature Standard
ECB – Electronic Code Book
ESP – Encapsulating Security Payload
FTP – File Transfer Protocol
HTTP – HyperText Transfer Protocol
IDS – Intrusion Detection System
IP – Internet Protocol
IPSec – IP Security
ICMP – Internet Control Message Protocol
KDC – Key Distribution Center
MAC – Message Authentication Code
MAC address – Media Access Control address
MD5 – Message Digest 5
MIME – Multipurpose Internet Mail Extension
NAT – Network Address Translation
NIDS – Network-based Intrusion Detection System
PGP – Pretty Good Privacy
POP – Post Office Protocol
RSA – Rivest-Shamir-Adelman
SET – Secure Electronic Transaction
SHA-1 – Secure Hash Algorithm-1
S/MIME – Secure MIME

SMTP – Simple Mail Transfer Protocol
SNMP – Simple Network Management Protocol
SSL – Secure Sockets Layer
TCP – Transmission Control Protocol
TLS – Transport Layer Security
Tor – The Onion Router
UDP – User Datagram Protocol
VPN – Virtual Private Network

Questions

(True/False)

A. Overview

A1   A threat will always cause damage to the computer/information system. _____

A2   Prevention of attacks is easy. _____

A3   It is impossible to prevent all kinds of attacks. _____

A4   Traffic analysis is an active threat. _____

A5   All attacks result in loss of data/information. _____

A6   Diskless workstations (with no hard disk and no full operating system) are not vulnerable to viruses. _____

A7   Auditing tools can allow or deny access to a network or computer. _____

A8   It is impossible to reproduce data streams based on the intercepts of electromagnetic emissions radiated from a computer. _____

A9   Integrity of data is not one of the concerns of cryptography. _____

A10   Validation of data is one of the concerns of cryptography. _____

A11   Hardware authentication is done in some systems by a specially designed chip which stores RSA encryption keys of the host system. _____

A12   Security vulnerabilities are not present in the processor hardware. _____

A13   The BIOS (Basic Input/Output System) cannot ask for a password at the start of the system. _____

A14   Message confidentiality always implies message integrity. _____

A15   Biometric devices cannot ensure exact matches. _____

A16   Use of biometric devices for authentication cannot have false negatives. _____

A17   Forgeries are impossible in biometric authentication systems. _____

A18   The *Bell-LaPadula* model addresses data integrity issues. _____

A19   The *Biba* model addresses data confidentiality issues. _____

A20   The *Clark-Wilson* model addresses data integrity issues. _____

B. Cryptography

B1   The algorithms used in encryption systems are usually published (publicly known). _____

B2   One-time pads are provably secure (unbreakable). _____

B3   One-time pads are commonly used in practice. _____

B4   The one–time pad is not practical for implementation. _____

B5   When all messages are distinct, but are of the same length, then it is secure to re-use the same one-time-pad for encryption. _____

B6   One-time pad is well suited for long messages. _____

B7   The diffusion property increases the difficulty of uncovering the key from the ciphertext. _____

B8   In any cryptosystem, some information in the plaintext will be lost upon encryption. _____

B9   In symmetric key encryption, confidentiality of the message lies in the secrecy of the algorithm. _____

B10   It is never the case that two different keys generate the same ciphertext for the same message. _____

B11   Symmetric key system cannot support nonrepudiation without employing a trusted third party. _____

B12   Stream (mode) cypher is better suited to encrypting files, emails, and databases. _____

B13   Stream ciphers usually operate slower than block ciphers. _____

B14   The unit of encryption in stream ciphers is usually small (Byte/Bit). _____

B15   Stream ciphers are used in file transfers and emails. _____

B16 Block ciphers are used in short data transfers between Web servers and browsers. _____

B17 The commonly used defense against brute force attack is using a larger key. _____

B18 The efficiency (computation time) of encryption/decryption is independent of the key size. _____

B19 A stream cipher can work on bits of data (one bit at a time). _____

B20 A stream cipher will not work on data more than a byte in size. _____

B21 Software implementation of stream ciphers is faster than those of block ciphers. _____

B22 The Data Encryption Standard (DES) uses several intricate and complex functions during the encryption process. _____

B23 In DES, the decryption algorithm is identical to the encryption algorithm. _____

B24 All rounds in DES are identical. _____

B25 DES has been broken due to flaws in its algorithm. _____

B26 A row of an S-box in DES may contain duplicate elements. _____

B27 No two elements in any row of an S-box of DES are the same. _____

B28 No two elements in any column of an S-box of DES are the same. _____

B29 No two S-boxes of DES give the same output for the same row and column numbers. _____

B30 3DES can be used to decrypt data which has been encrypted with DES. _____

B31   The underlying encryption algorithm in 3DES is different than in DES. _____

B32   3DES requires three times as many calculations as DES. _____

B33   3DES has three times the security of DES. _____

B34   In DES encryption, the original key is never used for encryption in any of the rounds. _____

B35   DES is considered weak due to known flaws in its cryptographic algorithm. _____

B36   DES is now considered weak due to its small key size. _____

B37   The CFB (Cipher Feed Back) mode of DES gives the effect of stream cipher. _____

B38   In the ECB (Electronic Code Book) mode of DES, an error in one cipher-text block propagates to other plaintext-blocks. _____

B39   In the CBC (Cipher Block Chaining) mode of DES, a bit error in plaintext block P_1 affects all the cipher-text blocks. _____

B40   In the ECB mode of DES, the same plaintext block produces the same ciphertext block. _____

B41   In the ECB (Electronic Code Book) mode of DES, the decryption of any block of ciphertext the C_i is independent on any other ciphertext block(s). _____

B42   The ciphertext produced by ECB mode for lengthy messages exhibits regularities corresponding to those in the plaintext. _____

B43   The AES supports different key lengths. _____

B44   AES supports plaintext blocks of different lengths. _____

B45   All rounds of the AES are identical. _____

B46   In AES, the decryption algorithm makes use of the expanded key in reverse order. _____

B47   In AES, the decryption algorithm is identical to the encryption algorithm. _____

B48   In the Mix Column transformation of AES, each byte of a column is mapped to a new value that is a function of all four bytes of that column. _____

B49   In the S-Box of AES, all entries are distinct. _____

B50   In the Inverse S-Box of AES, not all entries are distinct. _____

B51   The ranges of values in the S-Box and Inverse S-Box of AES are not the same. _____

B52   AES is a byte-oriented cipher (all operations are purely byte-level). _____

B53   In AES encryption, the original key is never used for encryption in any of the rounds. _____

B54   In Advanced Encryption Standard (AES), the 'shift rows' step contributes to confusion. _____

B55   RC4 is an example of a block cipher. _____

B56   RC4 is used in SSL (Secure Socket Layer) and TLS (Transport Layer Security). _____

B57   Public key encryption is much slower than symmetric key encryption. _____

B58   Public key encryption is widely used for encryption of data. _____

B59   Public-key system is commonly used in the distribution of secret (symmetric) keys. _____

B60   In Public-key encryption, message can be encrypted using any key in the pair and decrypted with the other. _____

B61 The public key system cannot be used for both confidentiality and authentication at the same time. _____

B62 RSA encryption works on blocks of input data. _____

B63 RSA cannot be used for (generating) digital signatures. _____

B64 RSA can be used for distributing symmetric keys. _____

B65 In the RSA key pairs $\{e, n\}$ and $\{d, n\}$, n (which is the product of two large primes) is publicly known. _____

B66 In the RSA key pairs $\{e, n\}$ and $\{d, n\}$, n (which is the product of two large primes) is kept secret. _____

B67 The Diffie–Hellman scheme provides public key encryption of messages. _____

B68 The conventional encryption itself could serve the purpose of authentication (in some cases). _____

B69 Encryption using the private key of a user does not provide confidentiality. _____

B70 Public key encryption is computationally more expensive compared to symmetric key encryption (for similar sized plaintext). _____

B71 Encryption using the public key of sender provides authentication. _____

B72 In public-key cryptography, encrypting the message using sender's private key provides confidentiality. _____

B73 In public-key cryptography, encrypting the message using receiver's public key provides confidentiality. _____

B74 In public-key cryptography, encrypting the message using sender's private key provides authentication. _____

B75 Elliptic Curve Cryptography (ECC) is a public key technique. _____

B76   The key size of Elliptic Curve Cryptography (ECC) is about the same as that of RSA (for the same security strength). _____

B77   Elliptic Curve Cryptography (ECC) can be used to compute digital signatures. _____

B78   Elliptic Curve Cryptography (ECC) cannot be used for distribution of symmetric keys. _____

B79   *All* cryptanalysis techniques attempt to deduce information based only on message content. _____

B80   The Diffie-Hellman scheme can be used to compute digital signatures. _____

B81   The Diffie-Hellman scheme is not prone to man-in-the-middle attack. _____

B82   The Diffie-Hellman scheme is used for encryption of symmetric keys. _____

B83   The Diffie-Hellman scheme is a public-key method for encrypting data. _____

B84   Diffie-Hellman scheme is a method for secure exchange of public keys. _____

B85   In a public-key system, the private key of a user is also known to the certification authority. _____

B86   In most public key cryptosystems, the encryption algorithms are kept secret. _____

B87   Nonrepudiation can be ensured in symmetric key systems without a trusted third party. _____

B88   There is no need for a trusted third party to ensure nonrepudiation in a public-key system. _____

C. Key Generation, Distribution, and Management

C1   A session key is a symmetric key that is used just once. _____

C2   A session key is (usually) never a private-public key pair. _____

C3   The cryptographic keys may not be stored in a separate physical device (ex. smartcard) rather than in the computer. _____

C4   In all of the public-key key distribution protocols, there is no need of a central agent. _____

C5   Public-key key distribution protocols are much simpler than those used in symmetric key distribution. _____

C6   It is never the case that two certification authorities (CAs) issue certificates for each other. _____

C7   Session keys require generation of pseudorandom numbers. _____

C8   Key exchange and authentication protocols are usually combined in practice. _____

C9   Key exchange protocols are based on public key methods only. _____

C10   Upon compromise of the private key of a web server, the key is revoked. _____

C11   Session keys (which are used for short durations) are usually asymmetric keys. _____

C12   Distribution of the keys is a major problem (impractical) with the use of one-time pads. _____

C13   The distribution of symmetric shared key among the communicating entities is a non-trivial task. _____

C14   A single KDC can work well for large networks. _____

C15   Public key system eases the task of symmetric shared key distribution among the communicating entities. _____

C16   Public-key cryptography is more commonly used for the distribution of symmetric keys among communicating entities, than for encryption. _____

C17   Public-key encryption is often used in the secure sharing of one-time symmetric session key. _____

C18   Public-key (asymmetric key) encryption is more commonly used for encryption of keys used in symmetric key encryption rather than data. _____

C19   RSA Tokens can be used multiple times during access control. _____

C20   The keys stored in the Trusted Platform Module (TPM) chip cannot be read by software. _____

C21   Random numbers are used in the generation of (temporary) session keys. _____

C22   Plaintext public key is susceptible to man-in-the-middle attack. _____

D. Authentication, Hash Functions, Digital Signatures / Certificates

D1   The size of the MAC (Message Authentication Code) depends on the size of the message. _____

D2   It is impossible for two different messages to have the same MAC (using the same function). _____

D3   The computation of Hash code (Message digest) requires a secret key. _____

D4   No two distinct messages can have the same message digest. _____

D5   In a good Hash function, the hash code is a function of all the bits of the message. _____

D6   It is possible for two different messages to have the same message digest. _____

D7   The Hash functions are irreversible. _____

D8   The Message digest serves as a check of message integrity. _____

D9   The Message Authentication Code (MAC) is generated using irreversible functions. _____

D10   The original message can be reconstructed from the Message Authentication Code (MAC). _____

D11   The Message Authentication Code (MAC) serves as a check of message integrity. _____

D12   Public-key system is also used in the distribution of secret (symmetric) keys. _____

D13   A single KDC (Key Distribution Center) can work well for large networks. _____

D14   Hash functions make use of a key for the generation of the hash value.

D15   The Message Authentication Code is of variable length. _____

D16   Message authentication can be achieved by the use of Hash function. _____

D17   The computation of Hash code (Message digest) requires a secret key. _____

D18   Hash functions do not require a key for the generation of the message digest (hash value). _____

D19   In several applications, the message is not encrypted, but sent in plaintext with associated MAC. _____

D20   The hash values of two different inputs using the same hash function H can never be the same. _____

D21   The Hash function is a *one–way* function. _____

D22   A Message Authentication Code is not part of a Kerberos authentication implementation. _____

D23   Kerberos uses a trusted third-party scheme for the authentication service. _____

D24   Kerberos is an example of a single sign-on system. _____

D25   Kerberos uses symmetric key cryptography. _____

D26   Kerberos does not provide end-to-end security. _____

D27   Kerberos uses symmetric key cryptography to encrypt messages. _____

D28   Kerberos provides access, authentication, and authorization. _____

D29   Session keys never reside on the users' workstations under Kerberos. _____

D30   Shared secret keys are never stored on the users' workstations under Kerberos. _____

D31   Kerberos essentially provides a trusted third-party authentication service. _____

D32   In Kerberos the authentication of servers to clients is optional. _____

D33   In Kerberos the authentication of clients to servers is optional. _____

D34   Kerberos does not detect password-guessing attacks. _____

D35   The *remote authentication dial-in user service* (*RADIUS*) network protocol provides client/server authentication and authorization, but not audits of remote users. _____

D36   *RADIUS* encrypts all traffic between the client and the server. _____

D37   There are applications which require message authentication, but not message confidentiality. _____

D38   Message authentication is required for encrypted messages only. _____

D39   Message authentication can only be done using public-key techniques. _____

D40   In keyed hash MAC two communicating parties share a common secret key. _____

D41   Although keyed hash MAC uses a common secret key, there is no encryption/decryption in any of the steps. _____

D42   HMAC uses asymmetric encryption. _____

D43   Digital signatures are more efficient than MACs for authentication. _____

D44   Digital signatures are not used for confidentiality. _____

D45   A message digest provides data integrity in addition to authentication. _____

D46   Secure hash functions are not subject to attacks. _____

D47   The collision resistance property of any (well known) secure hash function has never been violated. _____

D48   Use of public key certificates prevents man-in-the-middle attacks. _____

D49   The root certification authority (CA) cannot be an issuing certification authority. _____

D50   The certification authority (CA) can generate the private key corresponding to the public key of the digital certificate that it generates. _____

D51   The root certification authority's certificate is always self-signed. _____

D52   The root certificates of all well-known CAs must be kept by the browsers. _____

D53   During the validation of the digital certificate of a user, all signatures in the chain of trust need not be verified. _____

D54   The same set of classes for different types of digital certificates are used by the different certification authorities (CA). _____

D55   The longer message digest has lesser chance of collisions. _____

D56   Given the hash value of the message, the original message can be easily recovered if the Hash function is known. _____

D57   In a MAC-based authentication scheme, the communicating parties should establish a shared key. _____

D58   There exist hash functions which do not make use of secret keys. _____

D59   Message authentication code (MAC) is not a key component of Kerberos. _____

D60   Digital signatures are not susceptible to birthday attacks. _____

D61   A user sending the same message to multiple recipients must use a different digital signature for each recipient for authentication. _____

D62   Digital signatures require an underlying Public Key Infrastructure (PKI) with certification authorities. _____

D63   Public-key encryption is used for creating a message authentication code (MAC). _____

D64   When using a message authentication code (MAC), the communicating entities need to have a shared secret key. _____

D65   The algorithm/formula for computing the message authentic code (MAC) is kept secret. _____

D66   The Diffie-Hellman method does not provide authentication. _____

D67   Signing the original message is seldom done in practice. _____

D68   The size of message digest is dependent of the size of the message. _____

D69   Original messages can never be reconstructed from message digests. _____

D70   Use of message digests helps in detecting attacks on message integrity. _____

D71   All message digests are generated with the use of secret keys. _____

D72   The algorithms used in the generation of message authentication codes (MACs) are kept secret. _____

D73   The hash functions used in the generation of message digests (ex. MD5) are publicly known. _____

D74   The (once popular) MD5 Hash function has no known vulnerabilities. _____

D75   The Digital Signature Algorithm used in the Digital Signature Standard (DSS) cannot be used for encryption. _____

D76   The Digital Signature Algorithm used in the Digital Signature Standard (DSS) can be used for key exchange. _____

D77   A message must be encrypted before being digitally signed. _____

D78   Generation of a digital signature requires the public key of the receiver. _____

D79   Serial numbers associated with certificates issued by a CA are unique. _____

D80   Just the serial number is not sufficient to uniquely identify a certificate within a CA. _____

D81   DSS is used for encryption of keys in symmetric key cryptosystems. _____

D82   DSS is used for symmetric key distribution. _____

D83   DSS cannot be used for key exchange. _____

D84   DSS can be used for encryption. _____

D85   Digital signature provides confidentiality of messages. _____

D86   The private-public key pair is generated and assigned by the certification authority (CA). _____

D87   A cryptographic hash function produces different outputs at different times for the same input. _____

D88   Computing the hash using SHA-1 requires a correct secret key.
_____

D89   Digital signatures use public-key cryptography to provide both integrity and authentication. _____

D90   Hash functions (ex. SHA-1) does not use a secret key in computing the hash. _____

D91   The strength of a hash function against brute-force attacks is independent length of the hash code produced by the hash algorithm. _____

D92   Computing SHA-1 hash for a data item requires a correct secret key. _____

D93   A secure hash function will never produce any collisions. _____

D94   Digital signatures prevent the forgery of the messages by the recipients. _____

D95   MAC (message authentication code) provides both confidentiality and integrity. _____

D96   The secret key used for message encryption and the secret key used for generating the message authentication code (MAC) are usually the same. ____

D97   Typically, the hashed form of the passwords are stored on a server.
_____

D98   Since the passwords are hashed, it is impossible for a malicious entity in possession of the password file to gain access to a system.
_____

D99   Encryption of password that is sent across a network to log on to a remote system is not vulnerable to eavesdropping attack. _____

D100   Use of salt effectively increases the length of the password.
_____

D101   The rainbow table is a list of passwords. _____

D102   The rainbow table is a list of hashes of passwords. _____

D103   Password cracking using large rainbow tables can be made more difficult by using larger salt values. _____

D104   The length of the hash of password and salt has no effect in making password cracking more difficult. _____

D105   Use of random numbers in the authentication process defends against replay attacks. _____

D106   A virtual password is derived from a passphrase. _____

D107   A certificate authority that issues a TLS certificate to a site can decrypt TLS traffic to that site. _____

D108   The certification authority has access to the private keys of the users. _____

E. Software and Operating Systems Security

E1   Using buffer overflow vulnerability, an attacker can place malicious code in memory. _____

E2   Validating all input is one of the means of preventing incomplete mediation. _____

E3   Time–of–check to Time–of–use errors would not happen if there is no gap in time between a check and the corresponding operation. _____

E4   Undocumented access points in the programs are inserted by the attacker. _____

E5   A normally null–terminated string which is unterminated will not be a vulnerability. _____

E6   Even in a single user system (ex. laptop), the OS should enforce memory protection mechanisms. _____

E7   A fence register can be used for relocation of a user's program. _____

E8   Access control list contains one list per object containing subjects and access rights. _____

E9   Two users having shared access to a segment must have the same access rights. _____

E10   The default set of access rights is always recommended to be the rule of least privilege. _____

E11   Poorly written programs (ex. buffer overflows) could be causes of security vulnerabilities. _____

E12   The operating system access controls comprise administrative controls. _____

E13   The reference monitor mediates only a subset of accesses between subjects and objects. _____

E14   The reference monitor is called upon for every access attempt. _____

E15   Virtual machines cannot be used to provide secure, isolated sandboxes for running untrusted applications. _____

E16   Virtualization can be used to simulate networks of independent computers. _____

E17   Maintenance hooks inserted in applications for quick maintenance will not pose serious security risks. _____

E18   Preventing authorized users from making improper modifications to data is not a goal of data integrity. _____

E19   Fuzzing can typically expose buffer overflows. _____

E20   Fuzzing cannot typically expose SQL injection vulnerabilities. _____

E21   Fuzzing can typically expose missing authentication/authorization checks. _____

E22   Buffer overflow vulnerability can be exploited in CGI scripts. _____

E23   Buffer overflow vulnerability can be exploited in the Lightweight Directory Access Protocol (LDAP). _____

E24   Validating data input is not an effective method to mitigate buffer overflows. _____

E25   Validating data input is an effective method to mitigate cross-site scripting attacks. _____

E26   Fuzzing cannot allow an attacker to identify vulnerabilities within a closed source software application. _____

E27   A stack overflow vulnerability cannot be used for any form of denial-of-service attack. _____

E28   A buffer overflow could lead to corruption of data. _____

E29   A buffer overflow could lead to memory access violation. _____

E30   A buffer overflow cannot be exploited to force unexpected transfer of control in a program. _____

E31   A buffer is located only in the stack area, but not in the heap area. _____

E32   Many computer security vulnerabilities can be traced back to poor programming practices. _____

E33   It is not possible for a system to be compromised during the installation process. _____

E34   It is possible for malware to get into a system during the installation process. _____

E35   Certain bugs in programs will cause security vulnerabilities. _____

E36   All bugs in programs may not be security vulnerabilities. _____

E37   Large software systems cannot be guaranteed to be bug free. _____

E38   Configuration of the operating system has no effect on system vulnerabilities. _____

E39   Default configurations of operating systems are more vulnerable to attacks. _____

E40   Execution of arbitrary code at a privileged level cannot happen as a result buffer overflow. _____

E41   Mobile code is software that is executed on mobile devices. _____

E42   Compliance test (that tests the security measures in place) is a non-malicious attack against a network. _____

E43   Despite memory protection of a typical operating system, malicious code running in kernel mode can write to memory areas of applications. _____

E44   Buffer overflows are possible in every high-level language. _____

E45   It is impossible to prevent buffer overflows when the programming language does not provide safeguards for buffer overflows to happen. _____

E46   Some programming languages facilitate detection of buffer overflow problems at compile time. _____

E47   Buffer overflow attacks target only buffers located in the stack, but not in the data section of a process. _____

E48   There exist run-time defenses that provide some protection for already existing buffer overflow vulnerabilities in programs. _____

E49   Software developed using defensive (secure) programming never fails. _____

E50   Software developed using defensive (secure) programming does not usually crash abruptly upon encountering an error. _____

E51   Certain attacks can cause erroneous conditions in a running program. _____

E52   Eliminating buffer overflow problem would completely eliminate the problem of Internet worms. _____

E53   Eliminating buffer overflow problem would not completely eliminate the problem of botnets. _____

E54   A system configuration change has no effect on disabling a vulnerable service. _____

E55   Access control lists cannot represent everything that an access control matrices can represent. _____

E56   The Access Control List (ACL) rules are based on address, protocols and packet attributes. _____

E57   Network administrators cannot create their own ACL rules. _____

E58   *Security assessment* tests the security measures in place in a network. _____

E59   Log files related to security events are usually stored on the local machine. _____

E60   The log files related to security events are seldom stored on the intranet. _____

E61   The log files related to security events are usually stored on an offline storage. _____

E62   Penetration testing includes all of the vulnerability assessment processes. _____

E63   Penetration testing weakens the network's security level. _____

F. Malware

F1   Worm needs a host program to propagate. _____

F2   Worms do not need a host program for their replication. _____

F3   All viruses cause destruction of programs and/or data. _____

F4   Viruses cannot replicate on their own. _____

F5   Rootkits can *only* reside at the user level of an operating system. _____

F6   Rootkits cannot reside at the kernel level of an operating system. _____

F7   Rootkits could reside in firmware. _____

F8   How a virus spreads can be completely independent of the payload it executes on each system it infects. _____

F9   Viruses can spread to systems even with no Internet connectivity. _____

F10   Worms can spread to systems even with no Internet connectivity. _____

F11   Viruses   can   spread   even   without   user interaction/input/action. _____

F12   Worms   cannot   spread   without   some   user interaction/input/action. _____

F13   A Trojan horse cannot send out copies of itself. _____

F14   A Trojan horse needs a host program to function. _____

F15   Signature-based detection can detect new malware. _____

F16   Heuristic detection cannot detect new malware. _____

F17   While sanitizing files, antivirus software will never destroy the files or adversely affect their functionality. _____

F18   Trojan malware (usually) uses tracking cookie. _____

F19   Boot sector virus mostly spreads through removable devices. _____

F20   Multipartite virus cannot infect the boot sectors. _____

F21   Multipartite virus can infect the executables. _____

F22   Multipartite virus can get into a system via multiple media. _____

F23   Polymorphic virus is not easily detectable by traditional antivirus software. _____

F24   Polymorphic virus usually changes their signature upon replication. _____

F25   Trojan malware can self-replicate. _____

F26   Trojan horses replicate themselves, similar to viruses. _____

F27   Macro viruses depend on applications for propagation. _____

F28   A worm can infect a computer even without any user interaction. _____

F29   A virus can infect a computer even without any user interaction. _____

F30 A virus usually attaches to header files and propagates. _____

F31 A worm needs a file to attach to for it to spread. _____

F32 A computer cannot get infected with a virus by just visiting a Web site. _____

F33 Real-world malware may have overlapping features/capabilities of different malware categories. _____

F34 Most antivirus software run within the operating system (OS). _____

F35 A Trojan horse alters the IP address of the computer. _____

F36 A Trojan horse opens backdoor for malicious software. _____

F37 Worms can cause hosts to communicate with each other. _____

F38 Worms cannot perform port scanning. _____

F39 Botnets can be detected by antispyware programs. _____

F40 Rootkits cannot usually be detected by antispyware programs. _____

F41 Rootkit functionality does not require full administrator rights. _____

F42 A multipartite virus is a hybrid of boot and program viruses. _____

F43 Trojans replicate themselves like viruses. _____

F44 Viruses do not infect executable files. _____

F45 A virus cannot infect multiple types of files. _____

F46   There is no type of virus which itself is encrypted. _____

F47   Certain types of viruses can subject themselves to compression/decompression. _____

F48   All functionally equivalent variations of a virus have the same bit patterns / signatures. _____

F49   Viruses infect documents, but not executable files. _____

F50   A worm has the capability of executing a copy of itself on another system. _____

F51   A virus does not have the capability of executing (by itself) a copy of itself on another system. _____

F52   A worm does not have the capability to log onto a remote system as a user. _____

F53   A virus that attaches to an executable program can go beyond the permissions granted to the program. _____

F54   A macro virus infects executable portions of code. _____

F55   Malware code cannot be designed to only infect specific systems. _____

F56   Trojan horse programs can communicate data from the victim's computer to the attacker's computer via email. _____

F57   A computer infected with a Trojan horse program can continue to exhibit normal behavior. _____

F58   A computer infected with a Trojan horse program can deviate from its normal behavior. _____

F59   A Trojan malware only steals (sensitive) user data, but will not modify or destroy data. _____

F60   A malware will never have a nonfunctional payload. _____

F61　Malware is only capable of doing damage to data (corruption) but not damage to physical equipment. _____

F62　Some viruses conceal themselves using encryption. _____

F63　There is no rootkit which can execute in kernel mode. _____

F64　There is no rootkit which can intercept kernel API calls. _____

F65　Malware has never caused physical hardware damage to infected systems. _____

F66　Some viruses are capable of adding their code to that of executables residing on disk. _____

F67　All uses of spyware are illegal. _____

F68　A worm cannot propagate across computers without network(s). _____

F69　A virus can propagate across computers even without the use of network(s). _____

F70　Macro virus can change how the virus is stored on disk. _____

F71　Boot sector virus is self-replicating. _____

F72　There are certain file extensions that are likely to be associated with malware. _____

F73　All malware infected files can be disinfected. _____

F74　Antivirus software cannot stop all malware incidents. _____

F75　Presence of a virus in a computer can damage (or corrupt) data/files even if the infected host file or program is not opened/run. _____

F76　Macros used by word processors and spreadsheets are potential targets for all kinds of viruses. _____

F77　No virus can stay in memory (RAM) all the time. _____

F78   Content filtering may not effectively block highly customized malware. _____

G. Attacks

G1   There is no attack where an attacker can enter a system bypassing the authentication steps. _____

G2   A flood attack launched with a spoofed address will not consume incoming bandwidth of the attacker. _____

G3   Spoofing involves redirecting traffic by changing the IP record for a specific domain. _____

G4   A man-in-the-middle attack usually interrupts the communication between the sender and receiver. _____

G5   A man-in-the-middle attack intercepts the communication between the sender and receiver. _____

G6   Availability is compromised in a man-in-the-middle attack. _____

G7   There is breach of confidentiality in a man-in-the-middle attack. _____

G8   There is breach of availability in a spoofing attack. _____

G9   There is no breach of confidentiality in a DoS (Denial of Service) attack. _____

G10   DoS is an attack on the integrity of data. _____

G11   Replay attack involves flooding a listening port on a machine with packets in order to disrupt service. _____

G12   Replay attack is an active attack. _____

G13   Increasing the amount of time before the resetting an unfinished TCP connection mitigates DDoS attacks. _____

G14   Setting up filters on external routers to drop all ICMP packets mitigates DDoS attacks. _____

G15   Setting up a filter that blocks Internet traffic with an internal network address, mitigates DDoS attacks. _____

G16   ARP poisoning involves changing the IP record for a specific domain. _____

G17   ARP poisoning involves broadcasting a fake reply to an entire network. _____

G18   DNS spoofing involves sending a flood of ICMP packets to the host. _____

G19   DoS attack can be carried out at multiple layers of network. _____

G20   SYN flooding is an attack on availability. _____

G21   DNS amplification is an attack the integrity aspect of security. _____

G22   DNS query flooding does not come under the network layer DoS attack. _____

G23   Most commonly, sniffing is an active attack which modifies the data packets passing through a target network. _____

G24   Sniffing interrupts the data/message flowing in/out of a target (victim) computer. _____

G25   Sniffing is capable of capturing router configuration. _____

G26   Sniffing is not capable of capturing web traffic. _____

G27   Sniffing is not an attack on network availability. _____

G28   HTTP, being an application level protocol, is not susceptible to sniffing. _____

G29   SMTP, despite being an application level protocol, is susceptible to sniffing. _____

G30   POP and IMAP being application level protocols, are not susceptible to sniffing. _____

G31   In active sniffing, the network traffic can also be altered to carry out an attack. _____

G32   Protocol analyzers (devices plugged into a network) monitor traffic, but will not manipulate it. _____

G33   In a spoofing attack, the attacker does not actively takeover another system to perform the attack. _____

G34   Session hijacking takes place only at the application level. _____

G35   Session hijacking can take place at the network level. _____

G36   Spoofing attacks can be mitigated using IPsec for transmissions between critical servers and clients. _____

G37   Setting up filters on external routers to drop all incoming ICMP packets mitigates session hijacking. _____

G38   A telnet session is not prone to man-in-the-middle attack. _____

G39   Use of different servers for authoritative and recursive lookups helps minimize the effects of DNS poisoning. _____

G40   In a DoS attack, each packet can potentially be traced back to its source. _____

G41   In the ping of death (PoD) attack, a flood of well-formed packets is sent to the target machine. _____

G42   In the ping of death (PoD) attack, a single ping with a packet that is too large for the server to handle can bring down a target system. _____

G43   Even a properly configured firewall cannot prevent a SYN flood attack. _____

G44   Man-in-the-middle attack is prevented by using public-key certificates to authenticate the communicating entities. _____

G45   All the nodes in the botnet can be issued commands and remotely controlled by the originator of the botnet. _____

G46   Botnets are used for DDoS attacks, but not for spamming. _____

G47   In a DDoS attack using zombie computers, each of the computers usually acts autonomously. _____

G48   Attacks are only targeted towards Web servers, but not firewalls. _____

G49   In an ICMP echo attack where the source address is not spoofed, the attacker gets affected with a flood of packets. _____

G50   Use of spoofed source addresses does not make it any harder to trace back to the actual attacker. _____

G51   DHCP snooping is a type of attack using DHCP protocol. _____

G52   DHCP snooping improves the security of a DHCP infrastructure, while DHCP spoofing is an attack. _____

G53   All the spoofed (forged) addresses in most of the DoS attacks are valid addresses of real machines. _____

G54   Amplification attacks do not use spoofed source addresses. _____

G55   Amplification attacks are the same as reflector attacks. _____

G56   In the reflector attack, multiple replies (responses) are sent by a Web server (intermediary) for each original packet that is sent to it. _____

G57   In amplification attack, the original request is sent by the attacker to the broadcast address for some network. _____

G58   Every flooding attack uses spoofed addresses. _____

G59   All kinds of network flooding are due to attacks. _____

G60 Prevention of spoofed source addresses defends against DNS amplification attack. _____

G61 Prevention of spoofed source addresses does not defend against reflection-based attacks. _____

G62 In reflection attacks, the source addresses of the packets are spoofed with the IP address of the attacker. _____

G63 In the *ARP spoofing* attack traffic meant for the target host will be sent to the attacker's host. _____

G64 ICMP packets without spoofed source address of the victim are sent by the attacker in *Smurf* attack. _____

G65 SYN flood attack makes it impossible for the victim server to accept new connections. _____

G66 With some type of attack(s) it is possible to shut down a server remotely, without logging onto it. _____

G67 A keylogger can be used as spyware. _____

G68 Denial of Service (DoS) and spoofing attacks are possible in the network layer of the TCP/IP model. _____.

G69 Modification of DNS records results in misdirected traffic. _____

G70 Most *botnets* rely on existing peer-to-peer networks for communication. _____

G71 SQL injection attack requires database administrator privileges. _____

G72 SQL injection attack requires an SQL statement that need not always be true. _____

G73 ARP spoofing is a method of session hijacking. _____

G74 DNS spoofing is a method of session hijacking. _____

G75   A DoS (denial of service) attack will not compromise confidentiality of data. _____

G76   A DoS (denial of service) attack will compromise the integrity of data. _____

G77   The process of changing email message IDs to look as though they came from someone else is known as *spoofing*. _____

G78   The process of changing IP addresses to look as though they came from some other source is known as *spoofing*. _____

G79   SYN flooding is an attack on network bandwidth. _____

G80   SYN flood attack involves malformed packets. _____

G81   Packets used in an ACK attack do not contain the body (payload) of the packet. _____

G82   Cross-site scripting injects client-side scripts onto web pages. _____

G83   Cross-site scripting attack can be prevented by filtering all user input. _____

G84   The denial of service (DoS) attack attempts to obtain sensitive information from computers. _____

G85   Leaving a connection half open is a symptom of SYN flood attack. _____

G86   There are specific kinds of attacks which are targeted toward specific port numbers. _____

G87   Blocking incoming ICMP packets will prevent Ping scan. _____

G88   Blocking incoming ICMP packets will prevent SYN flood attack. _____

G89   Ill-formed requests are attacks on vulnerabilities of Lightweight Directory Access Protocol (LDAP). _____

G90   SQL injection is a browser-based exploit. _____

G91   Session hijacking is a browser-based exploit. _____

G92   Denial of service (DoS) attacks do not happen at transport layer. _____

G93   Denial of service (DoS) attacks happen only at application layer. _____

G94   In SYN flood attack, the connection requests will have attacker's source address. _____

G95   Spoofing a TCP packet is no more difficult than spoofing a UDP packet. _____

G96   The effort required in spoofing a UDP packet and spoofing a TCP packet are about the same. _____

G97   Spoofing a TCP packet is significantly more difficult than spoofing a UDP packet. _____

G98   Spoofing a TCP packet requires correct sequence numbers in addition to correct port numbers. _____

G99   Eavesdropping is not possible in a secure Ethernet network. _____

G100   Attacker can inject forged packets in a secure Ethernet network. _____

G101   A packet sniffer can monitor network activity and determine possibility of a DoS attack. _____

G102   The serial port of a computer is not a potential entry point for malicious code. _____

G103   Use of static mapping for IP addresses and ARP tables are effective methods to mitigate ARP poisoning. _____

G104   Networking devices and services installed with a default set of user credentials are easy targets for attacks. _____

G105   Backdoors are usually inserted after the system is deployed. _____

G106   SSID (service set identifier) broadcast can most likely cause privilege escalation. _____

G107   Application flaws are most likely causes of privilege escalation. _____

G108   A rootkit cannot provide escalated privileges (administrative rights). _____

G109   An attacker can do a successful port scan to determine the open TCP ports on a target host by sending packets that have a spoofed IP address. _____

G110   An attacker doing a port scan with spoofed address in order to hide its identity will never know of open ports. _____

G111   In IP spoofing, the source and destination addresses in the sender's IP datagram are interchanged by the attacker. _____

G112   Messages can only be sent from the attacker to a bot (malware), and not the other way. _____

G113   The purpose of the nonce is to defend against the replay attack. _____

G114   After a fix for a known vulnerability has been developed, it is no longer considered a *zero-day vulnerability*. _____

G115   The primary defense against many DoS attacks is to prevent source address spoofing. _____

G116   In the ciphertext-only attack the attacker has the least amount of information to work with. _____

G117   The propagation and activation of bots is usually controlled from a central remote system. _____

G118   A bot has its own distinct IP address. _____

G119 The denial of service (DoS) attack only exhausts the communication bandwidth, but not CPU, memory, and disk space. _____

G120 Anomaly detection techniques are well suited for tackling denial-of-service (DoS) attacks. _____

G121 Presence of worms and spreading of worms can be detected by anomaly detection techniques. _____

G122 The way a virus spreads is dependent on the payload it executes on each system it infects. _____

G123 Cryptanalytic attacks use mostly brute force than mathematical techniques. _____

G124 Malware transmission attack is carried out at the network layer. _____

G125 Scans for vulnerable ports are carried out at the network layer. _____

G126 Scanning (passive attack) is done only at the transport layer. _____

G127 Use of public-key/certificate authority will thwart a man-in-the-middle attack. _____

G128 An attacker cannot eavesdrop on the TCP connection and observe the sequence numbers on any network. _____

G129 In source routing, traffic can be directed through machine(s) controlled by attacker. _____

G130 The AH protocol of IPSec cannot provide protection against replay attacks. _____

G131 Cross-site (XSS) attacks can never be used to exploit vulnerabilities in the victim's web browser. _____

H. Network Security

H1   In link encryption, the packet body (payload part of message) is also encrypted. _____

H2   It is not possible for a packet to pass through TCP layer but get rejected by the SSL. _____

H3   Onion routing prevents any intermediate node from knowing the true source and destination of communication. _____

H4   With link encryption, the header of a packet stays encrypted even inside a switch/router. _____

H5   With link encryption, the header of a packet is encrypted/decrypted at the intermediary nodes. _____

H6   With end–to–end encryption, the packet header is encrypted/decrypted at the intermediary nodes along the route. _____

H7   With end–to–end encryption, the packet payload (body) is encrypted/decrypted at the sender/receiver hosts. _____

H8   With link encryption, the packet body (payload/part of message) isencrypted before sending out on each link. _____

H9   With end–to–end encryption, the packet header is encrypted at the sending node. _____

H10   With end–to–end encryption, the packet body is encrypted/decrypted at the intermediate nodes. _____

H11   The connectionless protocol usually uses more new session keys in a given time than the connection–oriented protocol. _____

H12   Port scanning is used to determine ports on a target which are running and responding. _____

H13   In VPN, the same header information of a packet in a private network can be used for routing in the public network. _____

H14　IPSec implementation requires changes to TCP, UDP, and Applications layers. _____

H15　TCP checks only for transmission errors and not for security related errors. _____

H16　For connection-oriented protocol, a new session key is used for each data exchange during the connection. _____

H17　In end-to-end encryption, the packet body is encrypted/decrypted only at the source/destination nodes. _____

H18　In end-to-end encryption, the packet header is encrypted. _____

H19　A *network-based* IDS also monitors activities within host computers. _____

H20　A *host-based* IDS does not monitor network traffic. _____

H21　A packet that has the same source and destination IP address is suspicious. _____

H22　The address resolution protocol (ARP) does not have any protection against ARP attacks. _____

H23　It is not possible to insert code by hackers into ICMP protocol which is just used to send status information. _____

H24　A network router creates a new header for each packet that it moves forward. _____

H25　The routing tables at the routers are based on MAC addresses. _____

H26　A router does not forward broadcast packets. _____

H27　A bridge does not forward broadcast packets. _____

H28　A router uses the same network address for all ports. _____

H29　Authentication header (AH) protocol provides protection from replay attacks. _____

H30   End-to-end connection takes place in the data link layer. _____

H31   IP protocol is a connection-oriented protocol. _____

H32   Thwarting SYN flood attack can be done by the use of SYN proxies. _____

H33   Packet filtering firewall cannot be configured to discard all packets using source routing option. _____

H34   Packets arriving from outside the network with source addresses of hosts within the network are very likely packets with spoofed (forged) source addresses. _____

H35   Packets arriving from outside the network with source addresses of hosts within the network are (likely) not part of an attack. _____

H36   TLS (Transport Level Security) makes use of certificates. _____

H37   TLS uses asymmetric cryptography to encrypt the messages. _____

H38   Both communicating parties of using TLS participate in key generation. _____

H39   A TLS session uses more than one key for data transfer data from a client to a server. _____

H40   TCP traffic can easily be filtered with a stateful packet filter by enforcing the context or state of the request. _____

H41   ICMP traffic can easily be filtered with a stateful packet filter by enforcing the context or state of the request. _____

H42   UDP traffic cannot be filtered with a stateful packet filter by enforcing the context or state of the request. _____

H43   SSL is not vulnerable to denial-of-service attack. _____

H44   SSL (or TLS) cannot by itself trigger a re-transmission of packets. _____

H45   It is never the case that (at a destination) a packet is accepted by the TCP layer but is rejected by the SSL layer. _____

H46   A corrupted SSL payload may still have a packet with a correct sequence number and TCP checksum. _____

H47   TCP connection initiation requests from an external host to a local host could be blocked by a firewall, while the returning traffic from an external host to a local host for its initiation requests is allowed. _____

H48   It is never the case that SYN-packets from an external host to a local host are filtered out, while SYN-ACK packets from an external host to a local host are allowed. _____

H49   In VPN, the body and header of a packet in a private network is encapsulated as a payload in another packet and new header is added before sending onto a public network. _____

H50   Tunnel mode IPSec is commonly used in remote-access VPN. _____

H51   Transport mode IPSec is commonly used in remote-access VPN. _____

H52   In the transport mode of VPN, individual hosts do not encrypt the packets. _____

H53   In the tunnel mode of VPN, individual hosts encrypt the packets. _____

H54   Multiple systems can never share a single IP address. _____

H55   Support for IPSec is optional in IPv4. _____

H56   Support for IPSec is mandatory in IPv6. _____

H57   Secure socket layer (SSL) is a connectionless protocol. _____

H58   In transport mode of VPN, IPSec encrypts only the packet payload. _____

H59   In transport mode of VPN, the headers are unencrypted. _____

H60   In tunnel mode of VPN, IPSec encrypts only the packet payload. _____

H61   The encapsulating security payload (ESP) part of IPSec provides confidentiality. _____

H62   The encapsulating security protection (ESP) of IPSec does not provide authentication. _____

H63   The Authentication Header (AH) of IPSec provides confidentiality. _____

H64   The ESP protocol of IPSec does not encrypt the IP addresses. _____

H65   Authentication header (AH) protocol of IPSec provides data integrity and data origin authentication. _____

H66   Encapsulating security payloads (ESP) protocol of IPSec provides confidentiality, data origin authentication, and data integrity. _____

H67   IPSec also has a protocol for the compression of packet payload. _____

H68   TLS uses a different keys for encrypting traffic in the client-to-server direction and in the server-to-client direction. _____

H69   A TLS client confirms the validity of a certificate received from a server by verifying that the server signed the certificate. _____

H70   TLS provides protection against TCP RST injection attacks. _____

H71   UDP does not use any encryption. _____

H72   DNS uses symmetric encryption. _____

H73   TLS uses both symmetric and asymmetric encryption. _____

H74   Port scanning does not use any encryption. _____

H75   ARP uses symmetric encryption. _____

H76   HTTP uses symmetric encryption. _____

H77   ESP encrypts only the data payload of each packet. _____

H78   ESP provides for integrity, authentication and encryption to IP datagrams. _____

H79   AH provides integrity and authentication for IP datagrams. _____

H80   One security association is adequate for bi-directional communication between two IPSec systems. _____

H81   VPN does not use the Internet protocol security (IPSec). _____

H82   Internet protocol security (IPSec) encrypts only the packet data, but not the header information. _____

H83   Internet protocol security (IPSec) provides protection against unauthorized retransmission of packets. _____

H84   Telnet is an end-to-end protocol. _____

H85   Internet Protocol (IP) is an end-to-end protocol. _____

H86   In an end-to-end protocol, the intermediate hosts are involved in forwarding the messages only. _____

H87   In an end-to-end protocol, encryption/decryption of messages is done at all the hosts along the path from the source to the destination. _____

H88   In a link protocol, encryption/decryption is done at each host along the path from the source to the destination. _____

H89   The SSL record protocol provides both confidentiality and message integrity. _____

H90 In SSL record protocol, the MAC (message authentication code) is computed on the message blocks before compression. _____

H91 SSL handles packet retransmission and reliable packet delivery. _____

H92 SSL does not authenticate the message to the recipient. _____

H93 An SSL record is always contained within a single TCP segment. _____

H94 Multiple SSL records may be sent in a single TCP segment. _____

H95 The sequence number in the header of a message is changed in transit from source to destination via several intermediate hosts. _____

H96 The time to live (TTL) field in the header of a message can change in transit from source to destination via several intermediate hosts. _____

H97 Port scanning can be done via a TCP connection request. _____

H98 Port scanning cannot be done via a UDP datagram. _____

H99 Encryption is a primary defense against sniffing. _____

H100 SSL provides protection against SYN flood attack. _____

H101 The secure socket layer (SSL) protocol is asymmetric (the communicating parties have different roles). _____

H102 The secure socket layer (SSL) protocol provides confidentiality, but not authentication. _____

H103 The secure socket layer (SSL) protocol always provides server authentication. _____

H104 The secure socket layer (SSL) protocol always provides client authentication. _____

H105 TLS typically only provides one-way authentication (the server authenticating to client). _____

H106 In TLS, messages are encrypted using public-key encryption. _____

H107 In TLS, the clients (usually) authenticate themselves to the server. _____

H108 IPSec encrypts only the TCP segment but not the UDP segment. _____

H109 Using IPsec a new SA will be established for each packet sent in the stream. _____

H110 In IPSec, all the packets sent between the hosts will use the established SAs with the same session keys. _____

H111 Retransmission of the same segment by TCP running over IPSec will have the same sequence number in the IPsec headers. _____

H112 IPsec at the source increments the sequence number for every new datagram sent by the source. _____

H113 It is never the case that the same segment will be sent within different diagrams with different sequence numbers. _____

H114 An open port always responds to a TCP SYN message. _____

H115 Secure socket layer (SSL) makes use of digital certificates. _____

H116 IPSec does not use digital certificates. _____

H117 Transport layer security (TLS) and secure socket layer (SSL) provide complete protection against traffic analysis. _____

H118 IPSec is below the transport layer and transparent to applications. _____

H119 IPSec is optional in IPv6. _____

H120 In Tor (The onion router), the IP addresses of the nodes are encrypted. _____

H121 In Tor, some nodes may not have an identifying IP address. _____

H122 In Tor, the only IP address visible to the destination is that of the final node (exit node).

H123 With the use of Tor, the packets arriving at the destination node cannot be traced back to the original source node. _____

H124 Even while using Tor, the Internet Service Provider (ISP) can determine the traffic contents and websites visited. _____

H125 An intercepted packet in transit in onion routing can never reveal the origin or destination. _____

H126 In TCP, data is sent unencrypted. _____

H127 There cannot be multiple IP addresses as response for a queried host name from a DNS authoritative server. _____

H128 TCP connection initiation requests from an internal host to an external host may not always be allowed by a firewall. _____

H129 TCP sequence numbers can prevent spoofing. _____

H130 While establishing a TCP connection, the client and the server share the initial sequence number (ISN). _____

H131 In some systems, the IP address of a device can change while it is still connected. _____

H132 Hosts using Dynamic Host Configuration Protocol (DHCP) on a wired network (ex. Ethernet) are immune to possible DHCP spoofing attacks. _____

H133 TLS is not (generally) used to secure DNS. _____

H134 DNSSEC does not hide the names that are looked up nor for their replies. _____

H135   HTTPS does not mask the IP addresses of the clients nor of the servers. _____

H136   SSL operates at the application layer. _____

H137   SSL uses implicit sequence numbers. _____

H138   IPsec will increment the sequence number for every packet it sends. _____

H139   An SSL handshake takes place before a TCP connection is established. _____

H140   Session keys are established between two communicating entities during SSL handshake. _____

H141   Authentication of two communicating entities (ex. server and client) is done during SSL handshake. _____

H142   SSL primarily focuses on maintaining the integrity of the data. _____

H143   VPNs can hide browsing activities of users and maintain anonymity. _____

H144   VPNs can mask IP addresses of users and maintain anonymity. _____

H145   There is always a one-to-one mapping of hostnames to IP addresses. _____

H146   Many hostnames may correspond to a single IP address. _____

H147   A single hostname may not correspond to many IP addresses. _____

H148   Changes to the local DNS settings by malware could redirect the user to malicious sites. _____

H149   When host *A* sends a SYN packet to request TCP connection to host *B* with a spoofed source address, host *A* can still receive the SYN+ACK packet from *B*. _____

H150   Using Network Address Translation (NAT), IP addresses of internal hosts of a network are not visible to outside hosts. _____

H151   SSL and TLS provide essentially the same end-to-end security. _____

H152   ICMP scanning is used for checking live systems. _____

H153   Not every running/live host responds to ICMP ECHO requests. _____

H154   VPNs facilitate preservation of privacy of its users. _____

H155   Network mapper is a tool that can be used for creating an inventory of services hosted on networked systems. _____

H156   Port scanner is a tool that can be used for creating an inventory of services hosted on networked systems. _____

H157   Protocol analyzer is an assessment tool for checking particular versions and patch levels of a service. _____

H158   Protocol analyzer is an assessment tool that reports information used to identify single points of failure. _____

H159   Vulnerability scanner is an assessment tool that reports information used to identify single points of failure. _____

H160   Network mapper is an assessment tool that reports information used to identify single points of failure. _____

H161   Port scanner is also often referred to as packet sniffer. _____

H162   Vulnerability scanner is also often referred to as packet sniffer. _____

H163   S-HTTP and HTTPS communicate over the same ports. _____

H164   Small key size is a vulnerability associated with SSL certificates. _____

H165   Outdated certificate revocation lists (CRLs) are vulnerabilities associated with SSL certificates. _____

H166   Network mapper is a software utility that scans a single machine or a range of IP addresses. _____

H167   Tool such as *WireShark* can detect the presence of malware in a computer. _____

H168   Reverse DNS lookup can be used to identify SPAM emails. _____

H169   SSL uses public key cryptography. _____

H170   Blocking all incoming ICMP packets cannot be done. _____

H171   The sender includes an index into the security association table in every packet. _____

H172   Link layer encryption is not appropriate for communicating parties without a direct connection. _____

H173   Adding security to the packets at the network layer requires modifications to the applications / application layer. _____

H174   Under IPSec, the packets are guaranteed to arrive at the destination in the order they were sent from the source. _____

H175   The ESP and AH protocols of IPSec must be used together on IP packets. _____

H176   The AH authentication of IPSec authenticates the entire IP packet (including the outer IP header). _____

H177   When using the AH protocol, the type of payload (TCP, UDP, ICMP, etc.) is specified in the AH header. _____

H178   With the ESP protocol, an intruder cannot determine the type of payload (TCP, UDP, ICMP, etc.) because the payload type is encrypted. _____

H179   Multiple systems can never share a single IP address. _____

H180   In HTTPS, URL of the requested document is encrypted. _____

H181   In HTTPS, cookies sent between server and browser are not encrypted. _____

H182   In HTTPS, the contents of the document transferred are encrypted. _____

H183   In HTTPS, the contents of the forms (filled in by user) are not encrypted. _____

H184   HTTP over SSL and HTTP over TLS are significantly different. _____

H185   IPSec works at the transport layer (TCP, UDP). _____

H186   IPSec can detect and reject replayed packets. _____

H187   SSL provides no protection against SYN flooding attack. _____

H188   A packet that successfully passes through the TCP layer at the receiver could be rejected by the SSL. _____

H189   A packet passes through the TCP layer if it has the correct checksum. _____

H190   Penetration test will never cause any disruption to network operations. _____

H191   Port scanners compile a list of all hardware present within a network segment. _____

H192   Port scanners test only for the availability of services. _____

H193   Vulnerability scanners check for a particular version or patch level of a service. _____

H194   Vulnerability scanners compile a list of all hardware present within a network segment. _____

H195   No connection can be established without specifying a username or password. _____

H196 ARP (address resolution protocol) does not require any type of validation. _____

H197 An ARP reply is added to ARP cache without any type of verification. _____

H198 Bastian hosts provide most of the standard services that are normally provided on a host. _____

H199 Host computers of a protected network are placed in the demilitarized zone (DMZ). _____

H200 The very essential servers (ex. Web server, email server) are placed in the demilitarized zone (DMZ). _____

H201 The return addresses in the headers of all packets leaving a network (intranet) using a proxy server are not modified. _____

H202 Onion-routing schemes (ex. Tor) use a distinct cryptographic key for each hop from the source to destination through the network. _____

H203 Passive eavesdropping is easier on UDP traffic than on TCP traffic. _____

H204 An Internet Service Provider (ISP) cannot link IP address with personal information (name, address, etc.). _____

H205 Individual users can connect to private networks at home and access resources remotely using *router-to-router* VPNs. _____

H206 In the ARP protocol a host can authenticate the peer from which the packet originated. _____

H207 In the HTTP connection data is never encrypted and sent as plain-text. _____

H208 *Telnet* which is used for remote login uses encrypted text messages. _____

H209 Secure Hypertext Transport Protocol (S-HTTP) operates over port 80 along with regular HTTP traffic. _____

H210   Data transfer using HTTP (hypertext transfer protocol) is unencrypted. _____

H211   In The Onion Router (Tor), the data traffic is subjected to layers of encryption, each layer controlled by a different node. _____

H212   The DMZ systems never face attacks from the internal protected network since they belong to the same organization. _____

H213   Security controls exist at each layer of the TCP/IP model. _____

H214   ISPs need to ensure that the packets going out to the Internet have addresses in the valid range. _____

H215   Application layer security mechanisms can protect application data as well as lower level information such as IP addresses. _____

H216   S-HTTP (Secure Hypertext Transport Protocol) and HTTPS (HTTP over SSL) are the same. _____

H217   Secure Hypertext Transport Protocol (S-HTTP) operates over port other than regular HTTP traffic (port 80). _____

H218   Scanning can be done at multiple (application, transport, network) layers of the network. _____

H219   ISPs (Internet Service Providers) cannot cache HTTPS traffic. _____

H220   Examining the source IP address is sufficient to determine where the message came from. _____

H221   Configuration of routers will not have no effect on vulnerabilities. _____

H222   In connection–oriented protocols, usually the same session key is used for the duration the connection is open. _____

I. Web Security and Application Security

I1   When a link to a Web server is clicked on in a browser, data from several other sites may also be loaded. _____

I2   Support for add-ins and plug-ins in browsers could cause vulnerabilities. _____

I3   The SET (Secure Electronic Transaction) is a payment system. _____

I4   SQL statements can be used by attackers to bypass authentication. _____

I5   A cookie is an executable script or program. _____

I6   PGP (Pretty Good Privacy) is a security mechanism for email. _____

I7   PGP (Pretty Good Privacy) does not provide authentication.

I8   After Radix–64 conversion (in PGP), there will be data expansion.

I9   PGP message is encrypted with a one–time session key.

I10   PGP (Pretty Good Privacy) does not provide authentication. _____

I11   PGP message is encrypted with the receiver's public key. _____

I12   The public–key ring (in PGP) of a user consists of the public keys of the user. _____

I13   The key ID in the private–key ring (in PGP) is the least significant 64 bits of the private key. _____

I14   *All* cookies are stored permanently on the hard disk. _____

I15   Some cookies are erased from the Web browser's memory at the end of a session. _____

I16   Rule-based access control is not necessarily identity-based. _____

I17   It is not possible to configure a database so users can or cannot see at the granularity of fields within database records. _____

I18   Decisions about access of objects are made solely on the identity of the subject. _____

I19   Decisions about access of objects are made solely on the sensitivity of object's content. _____

I20   Cookies pose the risks of personal data collection and impersonation. _____

I21   A cookie can keep track of every website that a user visits. _____

I22   Typically the only site which can access a cookie file is the site that created it. _____

I23   A cookie file only contains information about the user related to the particular site that created the cookie. _____

I24   A cookie in a computer can track all activities on it. _____

I25   A cookie in a computer can adversely affect the computer's performance. _____

I26   A cookie can sometimes destroy information in the computer. _____

I27   A user has the option to not permit cookies to be stored on the computer. _____

I28   Cookies could pose data integrity threats. _____

I29   Cookies could pose data confidentiality threats. _____

I30   Cookies pose risks of breach of privacy. _____

I31   Cookies are not required (mandatory) for all Web pages to work properly. _____

I32　Using a stolen cookie the account can be accessed from some Web sites without needing login details (provided the cookie has not expired or changed since it was stolen). _____

I33　The Simple Mail Transfer Protocol (SMTP) does not provide authentication. _____

I34　The Simple Mail Transfer Protocol (SMTP) provides message integrity check. _____

I35　The Simple Mail Transfer Protocol (SMTP) does not support non-repudiation. _____

I36　PGP does not provide sender authentication. _____

I37　PGP provides non-repudiation. _____

I38　Cookies may store authentication data. _____

I39　PGP provides confidentiality (via encryption), but not authentication. _____

I40　All browsers keep the passwords saved in them in encrypted format. _____

I41　The bytes transmitted by two web clients to the server when retrieving the same URL from a given HTTPS server will be identical. _____

I42　TLS uses the same key (for a client-server pair) for encrypting traffic in both the client-to-server and server-to-client directions. _____

I43　TLS provides protection against TCP reset attacks. _____

I44　Fetching a given URL over HTTPS takes the same amount of time as in HTTP. _____

I45　In SET (Secure Electronic Transaction), the merchant has access to payment information. _____

I46   Browser requests to the server never contain personal information. _____

I47   Web server response to browser never contains malicious (unsafe) code. _____

I48   A cookie is never sent from the browser (client) to the Web server. _____

I49   Typically, no Web site other than the one that created the cookie can read it. _____

I50   All cookies reside on the client (browser) until explicitly deleted by the user. _____

I51   Cookies can only be placed by Web servers that a user is visiting directly. _____

I52   Web servers in domains other than the one a user is visiting directly, can also place cookies in the client (browser). _____

I53   Browser (client) always send the cookie to Web server over HTTPS. _____

I54   In SQL injection attack, the malicious data goes from the server to the browser (client). _____

I55   Web application penetration testing can check for URL manipulation vulnerability. _____

I56   Web application penetration testing cannot check for SQL injection vulnerability. _____

I57   Web application penetration testing cannot check for session hijacking vulnerability. _____

I58   Web application penetration testing can check for vulnerabilities in web server configuration. _____

I59   Web application penetration testing can check for cross site scripting vulnerabilities. _____

I60   Web application penetration testing cannot check for buffer overflow vulnerabilities. _____

I61   It is not possible to configure client browsers to block all cookies. _____

I62   Disabling third-party browser extensions is an effective method to mitigate buffer overflows. _____

I63   Disabling third-party browser extensions is not an effective method to mitigate cross-site scripting attacks. _____

I64   Blocking third-party cookies is not an effective method to mitigate buffer overflows. _____

I65   Blocking third-party cookies is an effective method to mitigate cross-site scripting attacks. _____

I66   Tracking cookie is used by spyware. _____

I67   Cookies are executable files. _____

I68   Cookies are used for the purpose of spying on the browsing patterns of users. _____

I69   The primary purpose of cookies is to provide convenience to users by way of not having to retype several pieces of information while using a Web service. _____

I70   The data in the cookies can be used to reveal browsing patterns of users. _____

I71   Misuse of cookies may lead to compromise of privacy. _____

I72   Cookies cannot be misused for impersonation. _____

I73   The cookie is an executable file. _____

I74   The cookie is stored on the Web server. _____

I75   The cookie is stored on the client computer. _____

I76   A cookie can be associated with more than one Web site. _____

I77   The information in a cookie is never transmitted from the browser to the Web server. _____

I78   The information in a persistent cookie is transmitted to the Web server every time the user visits the website belonging to the server. _____

I79   A cookie, which is a plaintext file, cannot be misused as spyware. _____

I80   Just visiting certain (malicious) Web sites will download spyware on the client computer. _____

I81   Cookies can be used for authentication of browser clients. _____

I82   A stolen cookie cannot be used to impersonate the user/entity (from whom it was stolen). _____

I83   Pretty good privacy (PGP) does not use digital certificates. _____

I84   PGP uses a certificate authority to issue digital certificates. _____

I85   In PGP, individual users issue and manage their digital certificates. _____

I86   Certificates used in PGP can have multiple signatures. _____

I87   Every Web site on the Internet is visible to a search engine. _____

I88   Use of private window, or incognito mode prevents browsing history from being stored. _____

I89   In a null session the connection is authenticated. _____

I90   Cookies can be used to mitigate cross-site scripting (XSS). _____

I91   Clicking on something malicious on a pop-up window will not infect the computer. _____

I92   SSL provides encryption of server messages only. _____

I93   Provision of client authentication in SSL is optional. _____

I94   For public-key certification, PGP uses certification authorities. _____

I95   PGP uses public-key encryption for message encryption. _____

I96   Pretty good privacy (PGP) is not well suited for secure communication between a Web server and client. _____

I97   PGP uses public key cryptography to encrypt the messages. _____

I98   In PGP, compression of the message is done after encryption. _____

I99   In PGP, compression of the message before encryption results in faster encryption. _____

I100   Email filters operate on inbound email traffic only. _____

I101   Software updates are usually sent unencrypted. _____

I102   Software updates sent unencrypted are usually accompanied by message authentic code (MAC) to ensure integrity. _____

I103   Backdoors can be inserted during system testing and integration. _____

I104   Unremoved shortcut entry points inserted during code development to allow rapid evaluation and testing cannot be used to gain unauthorized access. _____

I105   A tracking cookie typically stays much longer than a session cookie. _____

I106   FTP servers support anonymous file access and unencrypted authentication. _____

I107   CGI (common gateway interface) scripts run on the client system. _____

I108   CGI scripts may be exploited to leak details about running server processes and daemons. _____

I109   While using an anonymizing proxy server, the Internet Service Provider (ISP) will still be able to see the URLs the web pages browsed by the user. _____

I110   While using an anonymizing proxy server, the Internet Service Provider (ISP) will not be able to see the contents of the web pages browsed by the user. _____

I111   Most of the transactions in e-commerce use only one-way authentication. _____

I112   In the e-commerce transactions using only one-way authentication, the business Website (server) has to authenticate the user (client/browser). _____

I113   Validation of input to remove hypertext prevents cross-site scripting. _____

I114   In S/MIME, the message body is not encrypted for every message. _____

I115   In S/MIME, the public key scheme is used for message encryption. _____

I116   The one-time session key used to encrypt the message in S/MIME is just a large random number. _____

I117   RSA public-key encryption algorithm cannot be for the digital signature of S/MIME messages. _____

I118   A malicious Website will infect all clients (browsers) visiting that site. _____

I119   Some Websites continue to provide their intended functionalities despite the presence malware in them. _____

I120   Despite the computer of the 'victim' being secure (not vulnerable), a drive-by download attack can succeed. _____

I121   A user has to download some files from a compromised web site in order for a drive-by download attack to happen. _____

I122   After a browser accepts cookie from a Web server, all future requests to that server will be accompanied by that cookie. _____

I123   Cookies can reveal personal information (name, address, etc.). _____

I124   Whitelisting by way of allowing only well-defined set of safe values can prevent SQL injection attack. _____

I125   Clustering reduces the likelihood of a single point of failure when a server fails. _____

I126   S/MIME (Secure/multipurpose internet mail extension) certificates are the basis of single sign-on applications. _____

I127   Post office protocol (POP) periodically checks the mail-box for synchronizing the latest emails with that of the server. _____

I128   Both HTTP and HTTPS content cannot be downloaded to browser while displaying in the same page. _____

I129   Unencrypted email when sent over an IPSec or TLS connection is protected during transmission. _____

I130   Unencrypted email when sent over an IPSec or TLS connection is unprotected in the intermediate servers along the way. _____

J. Firewalls and Intrusion Detection

J1   Default configurations of firewalls are more vulnerable to attacks. _____

J2   Firewalls cannot help prevent worms from propagating. _____

J3   Proxy server gateways can act as firewalls. _____

J4   A proxy server can be made to work as a firewall. _____

J5   Firewalls do not control the outgoing traffic. _____

J6   A firewall may be implemented in routers connecting intranets to Internet. _____

J7   A personal computer (PC) cannot be used as a firewall. _____

J8   The same machine cannot be used both as a firewall and proxy server. _____

J9   The headers of all packets leaving a network (intranet) with a proxy server are unchanged. _____

J10   A honeypot is always placed outside the external firewall. _____

J11   Firewalls cannot prevent all DoS attacks. _____

J12   Firewalls can prevent some DoS attacks by blocking all incoming ICMP packets. _____

J13   Any firewall can block every attack. _____

J14   A packet filtering firewall does not make use of information from previous packets. _____

J15   A stateful packet inspection (SPI) firewall can examine the actual contents of a packet. _____

J16   Packet filtering firewalls work well for small networks. _____

J17   Packet filtering firewalls are robust against spoofing attacks. _____

J18   Packet filtering firewalls cannot support the complex models of rules. _____

J19   Circuit-level gateway firewalls monitor TCP sessions. _____

J20   Circuit-level gateway firewalls do not filter packets individually. _____

J21   It is possible for an attacker to get past the circuit-level gateway firewall. _____

J22   A spam filter with *false positives* never blocks valid messages from being delivered. _____

J23   A spam filter with *false negatives* could allow invalid (undesirable) messages to be delivered. _____

J24   Bayesian filtering typically considers just the message content but not the message header. _____

J25   Packet filter firewalls cannot look at application-level data. _____

J26   Filtering outbound traffic helps control DDoS attacks. _____

J27   Some protocols use dynamically assigned port numbers. _____

J28   Protocols using dynamically assigned port numbers can be supported with a stateless packet filter. _____

J29   Packet filtering firewalls examine only the packet header information. _____

J30   Proxy servers facilitate more extensive traffic logging than packet-filtering firewalls. _____

J31   Proxies facilitate more intelligent filtering and control over traffic. _____

J32   Application-level gateways have lower maintenance overhead and performance penalty compared to packet-filtering firewalls.

_____

J33   SPI (stateful packet inspection) firewalls can detect several SYN packets coming from the same IP address and prevent SYN flood attacks. _____

J34   The filtering rules are applied *before* parsing the datagram headers by packet filters. _____

J35   Packet filters can defend against network mapping. _____

J36   Packet filters cannot defend against DDoS attacks. _____

J37   The default *deny* policy of a firewall is comparatively less restrictive. _____

J38   Whitelisting of spam filters has similar advantages as 'default deny' of firewalls. _____

J39   Spam filters configured to use blacklist is more restrictive than use of whitelist. _____

J40   With the use of whitelisting of spam filters, there are no 'false positives' (a genuine sender never gets blocked). _____

J41   With the use of 'default deny' in firewalls, there are no 'false negatives' (message from a malicious site is never allowed).

_____

J42   A firewall at the network perimeter will not provide protection against malicious insiders. _____

J43   Firewall on end host machine will not provide protection against outside attackers. _____

J44   A firewall will always allow returning traffic initiated by internal hosts. _____

J45   It is potentially more difficult to manage policies on firewalls at the network perimeter than on firewalls at end host machines. _____

J46   Stateful inspection is also called dynamic packet filtering. _____

J47   Improper configuration of a firewall could impact system vulnerability. _____

J48   Blacklisting is more restrictive than whitelisting in allowing connections. _____

J49   A stateless firewall keeps information about existing connections and TCP sequence numbers. _____

J50   Default firewalls are provided by some vendors with their operating systems. _____

J51   Firewalls need not examine each of the data packets that are leaving the internal network for secure operation. _____

J52   Packet filtering firewalls could be deployed on routers. _____

J53   Some firewalls can filter packets based on the name of a particular protocol (as opposed to the usual port numbers). _____

J54   Packet filtering needs to be done at the destination and not at the source. _____

J55   Every packet is not checked against the network administrator-defined rule set in the packet filtering firewall. _____

J56   Packet filtering technique could support the complex models of rules. _____

J57   Packet filtering technique is sometimes prone to spoofing attacks. _____

J58   Firewalls cannot be at the application layer. _____

J59   Firewalls cannot provide access control services. _____

J60   Firewalls can operate only at the network layer in the TCP/IP protocol stack. _____

J61   Packet filtering firewall applies a set of rules to each incoming packets only, but not to outgoing packets. _____

J62   The packet filter rules are typically defined on the fields of packet headers. _____

J63   The packet filter rules are typically not defined on packet payloads. _____

J64   Packet filter firewalls cannot prevent attacks targeting application-specific vulnerabilities. _____

J65   With the use of application level gateway, there is no end-to-end TCP connection between the hosts. _____

J66   With the use of circuit level gateway, there is end-to-end TCP connection between the hosts. _____

J67   Application-level gateways tend to be more secure than packet filters. _____

J68   Firewall functionality can be implemented as a software module in a router. _____

J69   The external firewall adds more stringent filtering capability compared to the internal firewall. _____

J70   Services available on the inside of a firewall are never subject to attacks. _____

J71   A firewall could consist of two or more systems cooperating and performing the firewall function. _____

J72   A packet filtering firewall typically only filters packets coming from the Internet to a computer (or a private network), but not the outgoing packets. _____

J73   Application-level gateway has additional processing overhead on each connection. _____

J74   Filtering of packets with spoofed source addresses can be more effective when it is done as close to the packet source as possible. _____

J75   Computers in the local intranet behind the firewall are not 'visible' to other computers on the Internet. _____

J76   Internet usage logs (audits) is not part of any firewall. _____

J77   Signature-based intrusion detection system (IDS) uses 'if–then' rules. _____

J78   Intrusion Detection System (IDS) is not effective in mitigating ARP poisoning. _____

J79   IDS allows identification of malicious activity after it has occurred. _____

J80   Rule-based intrusion detection is effective in detecting novel (previously unknown) attacks. _____

J81   Intrusion detection systems must cope with false positives and false negatives. _____

J82   Host-based IDS does not perform network traffic analysis. _____

J83   IDS (Intrusion Detection System) can be implemented as part of firewalls. _____

J84   Host-based IDSs (HIDSs) cannot detect both external and internal intrusions. _____

J85   NIDS (Network-based Intrusion Detection System) analyzes only network layer traffic, but not application layer traffic. _____

J86   NIDS analyzes transport layer traffic, in addition to network layer traffic. _____

J87   The deviations in the behavior of an intruder from that of a legitimate user cannot be quantified. _____

J88   An inline sensor monitors the actual network traffic passing through the device. _____

J89   A common location for a NIDS sensor is just inside the external firewall. _____

J90   Network-based intrusion detection uses anomaly detection, but not signature detection. _____

J91   Network-based intrusion detection uses both anomaly detection and signature detection. _____

J92   Host-based intrusion detection uses signature detection, but not anomaly detection. _____

J93   An Intrusion Prevention System detects bad packets, but will not block them. _____

J94   A host-based IPS uses either signature detection technique or anomaly detection technique, but not both. _____

J95   Anomaly detection is effective against misfeasors. _____

J96   Anomaly-based intrusion detection system (IDS) will never miss known attacks. _____

J97   Signature-based detection has the ability to potentially detect novel attacks. _____

IOIOIOIOIOIOIOIOIOIOIOIOIOIOIOIOIOIOIOIOIOIOIOIOIOIOIOIOIOI

Questions

(Sentence Completion)

A. Overview

A1   A weakness in the security of a system that may be exploited is known as _____

A2   A set of circumstances that may allow a vulnerability to be exploited is known as _____

A3   When both vulnerability and threat exist, then _____ exists.

A4   Reducing the damage due to an attack is known as _____

A5   Technique to make the attacks harder is known as _____

A6   Technique to make the current target less attractive is known as _____

A7   Getting the system back in action after an attack is known as _____

A8   Methods to handle attacks on a computer/network are known as _____

A9   Use of methods/techniques intended to break encryption is known as _____

A10   Cryptography and cryptanalysis are together known as _____

A11   The three main aspects/goals of computer/network security are: _____, _____, and _____.

A12   The three necessary ingredients before planning an attack are _____, _____, and _____

A13   Verifying that the subject is authorized to perform the operation on an object is called _____

A14   The components of *access control* are _____, _____, and _____

A15   Provision of _____ protects data from getting disclosed to unauthorized users.

A16   Provision of _____ protects data from modification by unauthorized users.

A17   Provision of _____ protects against denial of sending/receiving messages.

A18   Example authenticator(s) that a person *knows* are _____, _____, etc.

A19   Example authenticator(s) that a person *has* (possesses) are _____, _____, etc.

A20   Example authenticator(s) that a person *is* are _____, _____, etc.

A21   Example authenticator(s) that a person *does* are _____, _____, etc.

A22   _____ refers to reliable and timely access to data and resources provided to authorized individuals.

A23   The hardware, software, and firmware that provide some type of security protection are the components of _____

A24   An imaginary boundary that has trusted components (that make up the TCB) within it and untrusted components outside it is known as _____

A25   The components of the CIA triad in security are _____, _____, and _____

A26   Hiding data within other files/images is _____

A27   Masking of data in order to create data that is structurally similar to original data but is not authentic is known as _____

A28　Monitoring and keeping records of user accesses to system resources is known as _____

A29　_____ is the process of verification of the validity credentials of a user / entity.

A30　_____ is the process of granting of rights (permissions) to a user / entity to access system resource(s).

A31　Unauthorized transfer of data from a computer system is known as _____

A32　The *Bell-LaPadula* model was developed to address _____ aspect of security.

A33　The *Biba* model was developed to address _____ aspect of security.

A34　The *Clark-Wilson* model was developed to address _____ aspect of security.

A35　The model that requires that all modifications to data and objects be done through programs is the _____ model.

B. Cryptography

B1   The class of techniques/ciphers where the cipher text symbols are the same as plaintext symbols, but are at different positions is called _____ ciphers.

B2   The non–linearity of the encryption which makes it harder to determine the relationship between the plaintext, key, and ciphertext provides the _____ property.

B3   The property of the encryption which makes a change in plaintext affect as many parts (bits) of the ciphertext as possible, is known as _____

B4   The number of possible plaintext blocks for a block of size N bits is _____

B5   The key length in DES is _____ bits.

B6   The length of the round key (key used in each round) in DES is _____ bits.

B7   The number of Substitution boxes (S–box) in DES is _____

B8   The number of elements in each S–box in DES is _____

B9   The elements of S–boxes in DES are in the range _____

B10   The encryption which works on bit or bytes of the plaintext/input is called _____ cipher.

B11   In public key encryption, for confidentiality, the message is encrypted using _____

B12   In public key encryption, for authentication, the message is decrypted using _____

B13   Number of S-boxes used in DES is _____

B14   Each S-box of DES consists of _____ rows and _____ columns.

B15 The range of values of the elements of an *S-box* of DES is

_____

B16 Given that the input template to *S-box* 5 of DES is **1XXXX0** (where X = 0 or 1), and the output is **1011**, the actual input is

_____

B17 Given that the input template to *S-box* 3 of DES is **X1001X** (where X = 0 or 1), and the output is 0001, the actual input is

_____

B18 Given that the input template to *S-box* 5 of DES is **0XXXX1** (where X = 0 or 1), and the output is **1011**, the actual input is

_____

B19 Given that the input to *S-box* 2 of DES is **010001**, the corresponding output is _____

B20 Given that the input template to S-box 7 of DES is **1XXXX1** (where X = 0 or 1), and the output is **1101**, the actual input is

_____

B21 The number of new keys generated by the *expand key* stage of AES is _____

B22 The number of rounds in the encryption process of AES is _____

B23 The number of rounds in the encryption process of AES is _____

B24 The block size of data in AES is _____ bits.

B25 The key sizes of AES are _____, _____, and _____ bits.

B26 In AES, for an original key size of 128 bits, the size of a round key is _____ bits.

B27 In AES encryption, the number of rounds of processing for 128-bit keys is _____, for 192-bit keys it is _____, and for 256-bit keys it is _____

B28   In the substitute byte stage of AES, the output for an input byte of value 6B is _____

B29   In the Substitute Byte stage of AES, if the output byte is 4E, the input byte value is _____

B30   In the *forward shift row* stage of AES, if row 3 of the (4 x 4 byte) input is 4A C3 46 E7, the corresponding output (row 3 of the 4 x 4 byte) is _____

B31   In the *add round key* stage of AES, if a byte of input is 94, and the corresponding byte of the round key is 66, the corresponding output is _____

B32   Using public-key system, to ensure message *confidentiality* it should be encrypted using by the receiver's _____ key.

B33   In the _____ mode of DES an error in block number i of the ciphertext during storage/transmission affects only plaintext block i at the decoder.

B34   In the _____ mode of DES decryption of any block of ciphertext is independent on any other ciphertext block(s).

B35   In the CBC (Cipher Block Chaining) mode of DES, an error in block 3 (C_3) of the ciphertext would affect only plaintext blocks _____ and _____ at the decoder.

B36   In the _____ mode of DES, an error in a block i of ciphertext would affect only plaintext blocks i and $i + 1$ at the decoder.

B37   In the CFB (Cipher Feed Back) mode of DES, an error in block number 3 of the ciphertext during its transmission to the decoder would affect blocks _____ of plaintext produced at the decoder.

B38   In the _____ mode of DES, an error in a block of ciphertext during storage/transmission would affect all subsequent plaintext blocks produced at the decoder.

B39 In the CBC (Cipher Block Chaining) mode of DES, the cipher text output C_i of the ith stage of encoder (with encoding function E_K) is

_____

B40 In the CBC (Cipher Block Chaining) mode of DES, the plaintext output P_i of the ith stage of decoder (with encoding function D_K) is _____

B41 _____ is a block cipher in which the plaintext and ciphertext are both (treated as) integers between 0 and $N-1$ for some N.

B42 In the encryption using the *RSA algorithm*, given the two prime numbers to be $p = 3$ and $q = 11$, chosen (part of) public key $e = 3$, and plaintext message $M = 5$,

   i. the value of n (part of private/public) key is _____

  ii. the value of Euler totient function $\phi(n)$ is _____

 iii. the computed value of (part of) private key d is _____

  iv. the cipher-text C is _____

B43 Given that the *last row* of the state matrix of AES is **16 3E A7 8F**, the values after it goes through the *shift rows* stage of AES is

_____

B44 In the Substitute Byte stage of AES, the output for an input byte of value 6B is _____ (value in row number 6 and column number B of the *S*–Box).

B45 Given that a byte of the state matrix is 1C, and assuming AE to be the corresponding byte of the key, its value after it goes through the *AddRoundKey* stage of AES, will be _____

B46 The security of Triple DES is _____ times the security of DES.

B47 The two types of *symmetric* ciphers are _____ ciphers and _____ ciphers.

B48   The direct use of DES is known as _____ mode.

B49   In the _____ mode of DES, the ciphertext depends on the input plaintext block as well as the preceding ciphertext block.

B50   To send an encrypted message using public-key cryptography, the message is encrypted using receiver's _____ key.

B51   Using public-key cryptography, the sender can assure the receiver that the message indeed came from that sender by encrypting the message using sender's _____ key.

B52   In public-key cryptography, message confidentiality is provided by encrypting the message using _____ key of _____

B53   In public-key cryptography, message authentication is provided by encryption using _____ key of _____

B54   The technique that disperses the statistical structure of plaintext over the ciphertext is known as _____

B55   The technique which hides the relationship between ciphertext and secret key is known as _____

B56   A small change in plaintext resulting in a considerable change in the ciphertext is known as _____

B57   Any block cipher can be converted into a stream cipher by using the _____ mode.

B58   In the CBC mode of DES, the input to the encryption algorithm consists of the XOR of _____ and
_____

B59   In the _____ mode of DES, the ciphertext block for any given plaintext block is a function of all the previous ciphertext blocks.

B60   In (almost all) stream ciphers, the encryption operation (function) used is _____

B61 In (almost all) stream ciphers, the ciphertext (byte) is computed by applying the _____ function to the _____ (byte) and _____ (byte).

B62 In (almost all) stream ciphers, the pseudorandom key (byte) stream is function of _____

B63 _____ ciphers are used in short data transfers between Web servers and browsers.

B64 _____ ciphers are commonly used in file transfers.

B65 The scheme of a symmetric block cipher structure which uses the same algorithm for both encryption and decryption, and which is the basis of numerous symmetric key cipher systems, including DES, is known as _____

B66 The block size of plaintext handled by 3DES is _____

B67 Repeated application of DES to blocks formed by the XOR of the current plaintext block and the preceding ciphertext block is known as _____ mode.

B68 Confusion is commonly carried out through _____

B69 _____ is carried out by using transposition.

B70 _____ is the transposition processes used in encryption functions to increase randomness.

B71 _____ is the substitution processes used in encryption functions to increase randomness.

B72 Making each bit of the key affect as many bits of the ciphertext block as possible, is known as _____

B73 The goal of the substitution performed by an S-box of DES is to enhance _____

B74 Use of _____ ensures that two identical plaintext values that are encrypted with the same key will not result in the same ciphertext.

B75   The cipher which uses more than one alphabet to thwart frequency analysis is known as _____

B76   In AES, an inverse function is used in the decryption algorithm for the _____, _____, and _____ stages of the encryption algorithm.

B77   In AES, only the _____ stage makes use of the key.

B78   In an AES round, the most computation (complex operation) is performed in the _____ stage.

B79   In an AES round, the operation required in substitute byte transformation is (just a) _____

B80   In AES, the substitution box (S-box) is a table of _____ rows and _____ columns, and each element is of size _____

B81   The values in the S-Box and Inverse S-Box of AES are in the range _____ to _____

B82   The difficulty of breaking the RSA encryption is based on the difficulty of computation of _____

B83   The difficulty of breaking the *Diffie–Hellman* encryption is based on the difficulty of computation of _____

B84   In a public-key system, encryption with the _____ key of _____ provides authentication.

B85   In a public–key system, encryption with the _____ key of _____ provides confidentiality.

B86   The _____ and _____ modes of DES mimic (simulate) the stream cipher.

B87   The period of the Pseudorandom Byte sequence in RC4 is _____

B88   The key size of elliptic-curve cryptography (ECC) is (smaller?/larger?) _____ than that of RSA (for the same security strength).

B89   In public-key cryptosystem, it is computationally infeasible to compute the _____ key with a knowledge of the _____ key.

B90   Encrypted data that is produced by encrypting a bit (or byte) of data at a time is known as _____

B91   When the ciphertext gives absolutely no additional information about the plaintext, it is known as _____

B92   The essential operation done in the 'shift rows' step of Advanced Encryption Standard (AES) is _____

B93   The stage of symmetric key encryption where each element in the plaintext is mapped into another element, is known as _____

B94   The stage of symmetric key encryption where each element in the plaintext is rearranged (positionally), is known as _____

B95   In a symmetric key cryptosystem using a key of N bits, the number of possible keys to be tried on average in a brute-force attack is _____

B96   In a symmetric key cryptosystem, if the key length is increased by 4 bits, the effort required to break in a brute-force attack is increased by a factor of _____

B97   Random values, at least as long as the message itself, that are XORed with the message to produce ciphertext, and then discarded is known as _____

B98   The condition where that two different keys generate the same ciphertext for the same message is known as _____

B99   A function that is easy to compute in one direction (given x, to compute $f(x)$), but extremely difficult to do inverse computation (given $f(x)$, to compute x) is known as _____

B100   A one-way function which makes it easier to do the inverse computation given some additional (extra) information is known as _____

C. Key Generation, Distribution, and Management

C1   For _____ protocols, a new session key is used for each message exchange.

C2   The "number" which is used one-time during authentication / key exchange / key distribution is called _____

C3   The KDC in each of the domains in hierarchical key control is called _____

C4   In _____ key control, it is possible for the users to exchange session keys without the KDC.

C5   Public key encryption is commonly used to encrypt _____ but not data.

C6   Number of keys required in the node-level encryption of 100 nodes is _____

C7   Number of master keys shared between 100 hosts and a KDC (Key Distribution Center) is _____

C8   In hierarchical key control, each of the domains will have a _____ KDC.

C9   The number of session keys required for pairwise communication among N users using the Key Distribution Center (KDC) for the generation and distribution of session keys is _____

C10   The number of messages required for session keys distribution and mutual authentication between two users, using the Key Distribution Center (KDC) is _____

C11   Using the Key Distribution Center (KDC), the number of messages required for the distribution of session keys and for mutual authentication between a pair of users, for N users is

_____

C12   In public-key cryptography, for secure pairwise communication among N users, the number of distinct private-public key pairs required is _____

C13   In symmetric-key cryptography, for secure pairwise communication among N users, the number of distinct keys required is _____

C14   The *Diffie–Hellman* scheme provides the functionality of _____

C15   Use of _____ reduces the traffic to public–key authority.

C16   The Digital Signature (is very simply), encryption of the _____ using _____

C17   In the public–key distribution using key authority, the key distribution takes _____ steps.

C18   Session keys are derived from _____

C19   Personal computers and laptops come pre-loaded with the public keys of _____

C20   _____ chip is a hardware chip that stores encryption keys.

C21   Diffie-Hellman scheme is a method for secure exchange of _____ keys.

C22   Internet Security Association and Key Management Protocol (ISAKMP) provides a framework for _____ and _____

C23   _____ provides authenticated keying material for use with the Internet Security Association and Key Management Protocol (ISAKMP).

D. Authentication, Hash Functions, Digital Signatures / Certificates

D1   One-way hash function is also known as _____

D2   Each stage of the SHA–1 (Secure Hash Algorithm) takes input of _____ bits.

D3   The final output of SHA–1 after working on the entire input is _____ bits.

D4   The output of a Hash function, the hash value, is called a

_____

D5   The property of a cryptographic hash function where it is not computationally feasible to find two distinct inputs having the same hash value is called _____

D6   The property of a hash function H such that, it is computationally infeasible to find any pair (x, y) with $H(x) = H(y)$ is known as

_____

D7   The property of a hash function H such that, it is computationally infeasible to find $y \neq x$ with $H(y) = H(x)$ is known as

_____

D8   Use of authentication information within a trusted group of systems after positive identification of a user (without multiple logins) is known as _____

D9   The condition where two (or more) distinct messages have the same message digest is known as _____

D10   The number of possible hash codes of length b bits is _____

D11   The probability of a message not being hashed to a given hash code h among N equally probable hash codes, is _____

D12   The probability of two arbitrary messages not being hashed to a given hash code h among N equally probable hash codes, is _____

D13   Among k random messages, the probability that none of the messages is hashed to a given hash code h among N equally probable hash codes, is _____

D14   Among k random messages, the probability that at least one of the messages is hashed to a given hash code h among N equally probable hash codes, is _____

D15   Among k random messages, the probability that at least one pair of messages which hashes to a given hash code h among N equally probable hash codes, is _____

D16   Message digests are used to ensure _____ of messages.

D17   A message authentication code (MAC) is also known as _____

D18   Use of _____ reduces the traffic to Public-key authority.

D19   Public key certificate is verified using the _____ key of _____

D20   The list of digital certificates whose corresponding private keys are believed to have been compromised or lost is known as _____

D21   The chain of certificates associated with a given digital certificate is known as _____

D22   A self-signed certificate is also known as _____

D23   The digital certificate of the certificate authority is known as _____

D24   The public key of a user (system) that is digitally signed by a trusted third party is known as _____

D25   Certifying the ownership of a public key is done using
_____

D26   The entity issuing the digital certificates is known as
_____

D27   SHA-1 has a message digest of _____ bits.

D28   Requiring two pieces of information for authentication of a claimed identity is known as _____

D29   Number of messages required per user to get a public key certificate from certificate authority is _____

D30   Number of messages required for mutual authentication for a pair of users is _____

D31   Total number of messages required for pair-wise mutual authentication of 100 users is _____

D32   Centrally authenticating multiple systems and applications against a federated user database is _____

D33   While sending messages to multiple users, use of _____ is better (more efficient) than _____ for authentication.

D34   Nonrepudiation without employing a trusted third party is possible by the use of _____

D35   Data integrity is ensured for data sent between two IPsec-enabled hosts by using _____

D36   In practice, the _____ is signed instead of the original message.

D37   In the generation of message authentication codes (MACs), only the _____ is kept secret.

D38   The certification authority (CA) knows only the _____ key of a user.

D39 The recipient of a digitally signed message needs to use the _____ key of the sender to verify the digital signature.

D40 Generation of a digital signature requires the _____ key of the sender.

D41 _____ certificates are used in IPSec, SSL (secure sockets layer), and SET (secure electronic transactions).

D42 The most widely used format for public-key certificates is _____

D43 _____ is a unique integer value within the issuing CA that is unambiguously associated with the certificate.

D44 A system that stores the passwords of all users in centralized database and confirms the identities of users requesting services is known as _____

D45 The model upon which most remote authentication systems (both public domain and commercial products) are based is _____

D46 _____ chip is used for hardware authentication.

D47 The PKI implementation element is responsible for verifying the authenticity of certificate contents is _____

D48 The digital certificate is signed by the certificate authority's _____ key.

D49 Decrypting the hash of an electronic signature is done using the _____

D50 Unified use of separate identification and authentication systems is known as _____

D51 Combining information from multiple forms of authentication is known as _____

D52 The size of the hash code produced by SHA–1 for a message input of size 32 Kbytes is _____

D53   The hash algorithm used in digital signature standard (DSS) is
_____

D54   The signature of a digitally signed digital certificate is verifies
using the _____ key of _____

D55   The digital certificate is essentially the _____ key of an
entity signed using the _____ key of _____

D56   Digital certificates facilitate secure sharing of _____ keys.

D57   Pre-authentication of users before actually grating service to
desired services is done by _____ hosts.

D58   _____ could be considered a single point of failure
in *single sign-on* system.

D59   A trusted third party that holds their public keys of users and
generates and maintains user certificates, is known as
_____

D60   The number of bits in the hash value produced by SHA-1 (used in
DSS) is _____

D61   Verification of the identification information
(username/password, etc.) is known as _____

D62   A portable identity that can be used across business boundaries
allowing a user to be authenticated across multiple IT systems and
enterprises is known as _____

D63   Allowing a user to enter credentials one time and be able to access
all pre-authorized resources in primary and secondary network
domains is known as _____

D64   Most Internet service providers (ISPs) use _____ to
authenticate customers before allowing access to the Internet.

D65   Kerberos is based upon the _____ protocol.

D66   The common protocol schematic used for remote user
authentication is known as _____ protocol.

D67   The two broad steps used in an authentication process are
_____ and _____

D68   A graphical puzzle used as an attempt to distinguish input of human users from automated (software) agents is known as _____

D69   A type of challenge–response test used to determine whether or not the input/interaction is from a human user is known as _____

D70   DSS is used only for _____

D71   Some form of _____ protocol is commonly used for remote user authentication.

D72   Adding random strings to passwords before encrypting and saving them is known as _____

D73   Adding extra data to passwords so that identical passwords have different encrypted values (under the same encryption) is known as _____

D74   Use of _____ together with password increases the protection to dictionary attacks.

D75   A randomly chosen bit pattern that is combined with the actual password, before it is hashed and stored, is known as _____

D76   The file containing hashed passwords that is kept separately from the user IDs, is known as _____

D77   The table containing pre-calculated hashes of all passwords available within a certain character space is known as _____

D78   The _____ device synchronizes with the authentication service by using internal time or events.

E. Software and Operating Systems Security

E1   An undocumented access point is called _____

E2   The arguments, return address, and the stack pointer corresponding to a function call, stored on stack is together called _____.

E3   Passing more arguments than expected to a function, which goes unchecked, could cause _____

E4   The registers used by OS to ensure that the users' programs stay within their permitted memory space are _____ and _____ registers.

E5   The component of an operating system that regulates the access by subjects to objects based on security parameters is known as _____

E6   The part of the OS consisting of the fundamental and primitive operations is known as _____

E7   *Reference monitor* is the component of an operating system that regulates the access to _____ by _____ based on _____

E8   The architecture where every word of memory has extra bits to identify access rights to it is known as _____ architecture.

E9   The way in which a subject may access an object is specified by _____

E10   The security practice that is part of initial software development is _____

E11   Penetration testing performed by security professionals with limited inside knowledge of the network is _____ testing.

E12   The layer of the operating system which intercepts all requests to use of resources is known as _____

E13   The part of the operating system that handles all security related issues is known as _____

E14   The OS protection mechanism that mediates all access that subjects have to objects to ensure that the subjects have the necessary rights to access the objects is _____

E15   The part of operating system kernel that is invoked each time a subject makes a request to access an object, and enforces the access rules is known as _____

E16   Use of a collection of tools, techniques, and best practices to reduce vulnerability in systems is known as _____

E17   Adding protection mechanisms to programs/software to make it hard for attackers to exploit is known as _____

E18   Technologies used to specify which applications are authorized for use on a host are known as _____

E19   A controlled environment that restricts the operations that applications can perform and that isolates applications running on the same host is known as _____

E20   Code (software) that is transmitted across a network, to be executed by a (remote) system or device on the other end, is known as _____

E21   A virtual environment that allows for fine-grained control over the actions of code within a machine is known as _____

E22   A virtual environment that allows safe execution of untrusted code from remote sources is known as _____

E23   Giving programs and users nothing more than the minimal amount of privilege needed to function correctly, is known as _____

E24 List containing the mapping of users to access rights of resources is known as _____

E25 A framework that specifies how subjects access objects is known as _____

E26 Reference monitor is enforced by the _____ part of the operating system.

E27 Every access request of a subject for an object, the rules of the access control model are checked by the _____

E28 To determine if the request of a subject for an object is allowed is determined by the rules specified in the _____

E29 Users are not allowed to determine the access of objects by subjects in the _____ model.

E30 In the *mandatory access control* (*MAC*) model, the access/security policy is enforced by _____

E31 A centrally administrated set of controls to determine how subjects   and   objects   interact   is   used   in   the _____ model.

E32 *Rule-based* access control which uses specific rules indicating the access rights of subjects to objects is an access control (technology / policy) _____

E33 _____ are mechanisms used to restrict access by users to data contained in databases.

E34 _____ is bound to an object and indicates the set of subjects that can access the object and the operations they can perform.

E35 _____ is bound to a subject and indicates the set of objects that the subject can access and the operations it can perform.

E36   A matrix of subjects (usually in rows) and objects (usually in columns) and the entries containing access rights is known as

_____

E37   In _____ access control, access to objects is determined by the content within the object.

E38   Extra spaces inserted between critical regions in the address space of a processes to prevent buffer overflow attacks, are known as

_____

E39   The process of designing and implementing software so that it continues to function even when under attack is known as

_____

E40   A _____ security system processes data at different classifications (security levels), and supports users with different clearances (security levels).

E41   The facility used during software development which enables code to be executed without the usual security checks is known as

_____

E42   Legitimate backdoors used by programmers to debug and test programs are known as _____

E43   Organizing subjects in rows and objects in columns and the cells containing access rights in a matrix, is known as

_____

E44   Use of rules and criteria to make a determination of operations that a subject can carry out on objects is known as _____

E45   Reviewing a piece of code without actually running it is called

_____

E46   Actually running the code, observing, and studying the behavior is called _____

E47   The technique of providing invalid, unexpected, or random data as input to a program is known as _____

E48   Software testing technique that uses large amounts of randomly generated data as inputs to a program to determine its robustness is known as _____

E49   Feeding a target system with automatically generated malformed data designed to trigger implementation flaws is known as _____

E50   Access control is usually performed by _____

E51   The most common phase during which backdoors are inserted is _____

E52   _____ allow a user to pass a permission to another user.

E53   In the context of access control, possession of data which proves authorization to access a resource is known as a _____

E54   _____ make it easier to revoke a specific permission of a specific user.

E55   The _____ access control model is user-directed.

E56   The rules specifying which subjects can access specific resources can be set by the owner of the resources in the _____ access control model.

E57   Methodical probing of the target in order to identify weaknesses is known as _____

E58   The two control policies used to protect relational databases are _____ and _____

E59   _____ is a standard for representing vulnerability information.

E60   A non-malicious attack against a network that is intended to test the security measures in place is known as _____

E61   Access control technologies commonly used to protect copyright material is known as _____

E62   A less-secure channel via which the data written to storage is allowed to be read, is known as _____

F. Malware

F1   _____ virus hides signs that it has infected the system.

F2   _____ virus has the capability to hide from operating system or anti-virus software.

F3   _____ virus has the capability to hide by making changes to file sizes or directory structure.

F4   _____ is a type virus which tries to attack and disable the anti-virus application running on the computer.

F5   _____ virus changes its appearance.

F6   _____ virus usually changes signature upon replication.

F7   _____ virus is capable of changing its code every time it infects a different system.

F8   Example(s) of source code / text file that could be infected by viruses is/are _____ , _____

F9   The typical phases in the lifetime of a typical virus are _____ , _____ , _____ , and _____

F10   The actual function of the virus is performed in the _____ phase.

F11   The _____ virus can affect both the boot sector and the program files at the same time.

F12   The functionality of virus remains same but its signature is changed in a _____ virus.

F13   Malicious code installed in the most privileged part (root) of the operating system is known as _____

F14   A collection of tools used by a malicious user to mask intrusion and gain administrative-level access to a computer is known as _____

F15   _____ conceal malware and/or prevent malicious programs being detected.

F16   Boot sector virus infects the _____

F17   A legitimate file with a masked virus is known as _____

F18   The most common method of virus propagation is _____

F19   A special type of polymorphic virus that completely rewrites itself periodically is known as _____ virus.

F20   The virus which performs its malicious activity sporadically is known as _____

F21   The virus that attacks the computer in multiple ways is known as _____ virus.

F22   The software that records activities on the computer are known as _____

F23   The most common way for a spyware to get into a computer is via _____

F24   _____ is software that communicates information from a user's system to a malicious entity without knowledge of the user.

F25   _____ are malicious programs disguised as useful applications.

F26   The stage/phase when the virus is idle is known as _____

F27   The stage/phase when the virus function is performed is known as _____

F28   The stage/phase when the virus is multiplying and replicating itself is known as _____

F29   The stage/phase when the virus is activated to perform its intended function is known as _____

F30   The attack that uses multiple methods of infection and/or propagation is known as _____

F31   The malware used to capture keystrokes on the infected machine to gather sensitive information is known as _____

F32   Virus that stays in memory (RAM) all the time, is known as _____ virus.

F33   Malware which encrypts user's data, and demands payment in exchange for the key needed to recover the data is known as

_____

F34   _____ viruses vary the sequence of their instructions by including bogus instructions with other useful instructions.

F35   A _____ virus has the capability to change its own code.

F36   In the context of virus detection, *signature-based* detection also called _____ detection.

F37   The technique that analyzes the overall structure of the malicious code, evaluates the coded instructions and logic functions is known as _____ detection.

F38   Hidden entry points in a system that are set to bypass security measures are known as _____

F39   Part of a virus that helps in performing malicious activities is the

_____

F40   Software that records the keystrokes on a keyboard is called

_____

F41   A virus usually attaches to _____ files and propagates.

F42   The virus scanning that uses complex rules to define what is / is not a virus is known as _____ scanning.

F43   File with a list of known viruses, their sizes, properties, and behavior is known as _____

F44   Antivirus programs will be most effective when _____ files are kept up-to-date.

F45   The most commonly used technical control for malware threat mitigation is _____

F46   The kind of virus that changes its own code, making it harder to detect with antivirus software is known as _____

F47   The most common way for a virus scanner to recognize a virus is look for known virus attributes in the _____

F48   Comparing executable files with bit patterns of known viruses is known as _____

F49   Antivirus signatures are essentially _____

F50   Virus scanners look for _____ which are associated with some pattern(s) associated with a virus.

G. Attacks

G1 Use of random numbers in the authentication process defends against _____ attacks.

G2 Capturing packets, and then placing packets back on the network is known as _____ attack.

G3 A form of social engineering where an intruder pretends as a legitimate user and gathers sensitive information from (gullible) users is known as _____

G4 A security threat where an attacker falsifies the IP address of a server in the packet header is known as _____

G5 Attempt at breaking passwords by (automatically) trying every word in the dictionary, encrypting and comparing with stored passwords is known as _____ attack.

G6 A threat (attack) combining the characteristics of several attacks such as a virus, worm, Trojans, etc., is known as _____

G7 The attack where the user is tricked into revealing sensitive information or taking unsafe action, is known as _____ attack.

G8 A process for preventing session creation through a particular port is known as _____

G9 A bot server or controller together with one or more client-bots is known as _____

G10 The infected computers in the botnet connection are called _____

G11 The attack which overwhelms the server with a surge of requests more than the server can handle is known as _____ attack.

G12 A DoS attack coming from a large number of IP addresses is known as _____ attack.

G13   UDP flooding is an attack on the _____ aspect of security.

G14   Monitoring (and capturing) data packets passing through a target network is known as _____

G15   Sniffing involves data (interception? / interruption?) _____

G16   The most commonly used session hijacking attack is _____

G17   Attack where malicious code/script is injected into a Web application (Web page) using vulnerability in a Web site is known as _____

G18   DNS cache poisoning is also known as _____

G19   The attack which uses DNS vulnerabilities for diverting the traffic away from genuine servers is known as _____

G20   _____ should be blocked at the network perimeter to prevent host enumeration by sweep devices.

G21   _____ results in incorrect hardware (MAC) addresses corresponding to IP addresses.

G22   Attack using the vulnerability that has been found but not yet known to the application creator/owner is known as _____

G23   Vulnerability that has been identified for which there is no known fix yet, is known as _____

G24   Getting several Internet routers to attack a target server/system is known as _____ attack.

G25   In the distributed reflection DoS attack, connection requests are sent to several routers such that they have the IP address of _____

G26   SYN flood attack is a form of _____ attack.

G27   The Smurf attack is a form of _____ attack.

G28   Sending fragmented messages in a way which makes it impossible to reassemble them without destroying the individual packet headers is known as _____ attack.

G29   A DoS attack that is launched simultaneously from several machines is known as _____ attack.

G30   Systematic probing of ports to determine which ones are open is known as _____

G31   Checking to see if a system is vulnerable to specific attack(s) is known as _____

G32   Passing (undesired) Structured Query Language (SQL) commands and making a web site to execute them is known as

    _____

G33   A bad web site sending innocent victim a script that steals information from a good web site is known as _____

G34   An attack which modifies the cookie file is called

    _____

G35   Unauthorized access of information from a Bluetooth device is known as _____

G36   Attack where attacker's MAC address is substituted for victim's MAC address is known as _____

G37   The sequence numbers used in packets thwart the _____ attack.

G38   Nonces are often used to prevent the _____ attack.

G39   Time stamps / counters are often used to prevent the _____ attack.

G40   Replay attacks are prevented by the use of _____

G41   Man-in-the-middle attack is prevented by the use of _____

G42   Modifying the DNS server entry such that connection requests are redirected to the attacker posing as trusted host is known as _____

G43   Sending an email using a different name in the sender field, impersonating a legitimate user is known as _____

G44   Attack using a script inserted in the cookie file is known as _____ attack.

G45   SYN flood attack exploits the _____ part of the TCP protocol.

G46   _____ attack exploits the IP sequencing/reassembly part of the TCP protocol.

G47   Sending a number of connection requests in excess of that a system can handle is known as _____ attack.

G48   Malware that is dormant until a particular date/time is known as _____

G49   Malware that triggers action when a predetermined condition occurs is known as _____

G50   The _____ attack sends a series of IP packet fragments with confusing offsets.

G51   The attack where port 80 is overwhelmed with reload requests is known as _____

G52   DNS server resolves a host name into an incorrect IP address in the _____ attack.

G53   Associating the attacker's host MAC (Media Access Control) address with the IP address of a target (legitimate) host is done in _____ attack.

G54   Improper (attacker's) IP address is associated with a genuine domain name in the _____ attack.

G55   Determining the operating system (OS) that is running on a remote computer is known as _____

G56   MAC Address spoofing is a vulnerability at the _____ layer.

G57   IP Address spoofing is a vulnerability at the _____ layer.

G58   In a _____ attack using zombie computers, each of the computers is usually remotely controlled by the attacker.

G59   An attack where numerous SYN packets with spoofed (fake) source addresses are to a server is known as _____

G60   In a _____ attack, the ACK packet is never sent back to the server if the spoofed source address is non-existent.

G61   DNS protocol attack is done in the _____ layer of the TCP/IP model.

G62   Misdirecting user traffic by modifying DNS records is known as _____ attack.

G63   The attack where packets are captured by sniffers, information is extracted, and then placed back on the network, is known as _____attack.

G64   Tricking a device into thinking that an incorrect IP address is related to a MAC address is known as _____

G65   The host hijacked by an attacker to carry out attacks on the victim is known as _____

G66   Programs written to perform repetitive tasks on the Web are usually known as _____

G67   _____ facilitates a user/entity to pretend to be someone/something else.

G68   Using forged source addresses is known as _____

G69   The attack that sends ICMP packets to the broadcast address of a network with spoofed source address to be from the victim's computer is known as _____

G70   Using different keys for encryption for the different directions of a communication channel prevent _____

G71   A web attack in which a script is embedded in a URL such that when a Web server processes the URL, its reply includes the script within it, is known as _____

G72   The computers (servers) which are made to send responses to target (victim) clients to the spoofed requests sent by the attacker are known as _____

G73   Packets generated in response to a DoS attack with a forged (spoofed) random source addresses is known as _____

G74   In _____ attack, multiple replies (responses) are sent by a Web server (intermediary) for each original packet that is sent to it.

G75   In amplification attack the original request is sent by the attacker to the _____ address for some network.

G76   Not allowing directed broadcasts to be routed into a network from outside is good defense against _____ attack.

G77   The process of changing email message IDs to look as though they came from someone else is known as _____

G78   Making many connection attempts using spoofed source addresses and incomplete handshakes is a sign of _____ attack.

G79   Excessive traffic on the front-end servers that balance incoming requests among multiple back-end processing servers is a symptom of _____ attack.

G80   Continuous sending of ACK packets towards a target is known as _____ attack.

G81   A DDoS attack that floods the target system with a large amount of spoofed UDP traffic to a router's broadcast address is known as _____

G82   Connection requests rerouted to a malicious Web server is a sign of _____ attack.

G83   IDS (Intrusion Detection System) logs of incoming malformed packets is a sign of _____ attack.

G84   The attack where capturing the traffic from a legitimate session and replaying it with the goal of masquerading as an authenticated user is known as _____

G85   Technique where bots follow all links on the Web site in a recursive way starting from a given HTTP link, is known as _____

G86   The ICMP echo response packets generated in response to a ping flood using randomly spoofed source addresses is known as _____ traffic.

G87   Sending a series of malicious packets to a server is known as _____

G88   An attack that overwhelms Web servers with numerous HTTP requests is known as _____

G89   In reflection attacks, the source addresses of the packets are spoofed with the IP address of the _____

G90   Sending a series of DNS requests containing the spoofed source address for the target system is known as _____ attack.

G91   The attack which uses incorrect handling/checking of program input data to influence the flow of execution of the program is known as _____

G92   Using the unchecked/incorrectly checked input to construct a malicious command that is subsequently executed by the system with the privileges of the attacked program is known as _____ attack.

G93   The attack where the input includes code that is subsequently executed by the target system (victim) is known as _____ attack.

G94   The attack which makes use of assignment of global variables to field values in Web forms is known as _____ attack.

G95   The attack where user supplied input is used to construct a SQL request to retrieve information from a database is known as

_____

G96   The reachable and exploitable vulnerabilities in a system are known as _____

G97   The attack which collects an infected user's clicks is known as _____

G98   The attack where a bot starts from a given HTTP link and follows all links on the provided Web site is known as

_____

G99   Recursive HTTP attack is also known as _____

G100   An already planted malicious script in one of the pages of an insecure web sites installing a malware directly onto the computer of someone who visits the site, is known as _____

G101   Simply visiting a Web site containing malicious script via a vulnerable browser (client) can result in a _____ attack.

G102   Password guessing attack is carried out at the _____ layer of the network.

G103   SYN flood attacks are carried out at the _____ layer of the network.

G104   Scans for vulnerable ports are carried out at the _____ layer.

G105   Attacks using spoofed IP addresses are carried out at the _____ layer.

G106   Attacks using illegal IP header values are carried out at the _____ layer.

G107   An attacker sending a flood of malformed or malicious pings to a computer is known as _____ attack.

G108   Reassembly of malformed packet fragments resulting in an oversized packet, leading to buffer overflow is known as _____ attack.

G109   Sending a stream of ICMP Echo Request (ping) packets without waiting for replies is known as _____ attack.

G110   A DoS / DDoS attack that floods a target with user datagram protocol (UDP) packets is known as _____

G111   The attack where actual database commands are inserted in place of valid input, which are run by the application is known as

        _____

G112   The denial of service (DoS) attack on the Web is an attack on the _____ aspect of the CIA triad.

G113   In a Distributed Denial of Service (DDoS) attack with N Zombies, each with a connection bandwidth of W bps (bits/sec), and the target machine with a connection bandwidth of X bps, the required condition for the attack to succeed is _____

G114   In the _____ attack, the encryption algorithm and ciphertext are known to the cryptanalyst.

G115   In the _____ attack, the encryption algorithm, ciphertext, and one or more plaintext-ciphertext pairs are known to the cryptanalyst.

G116   Several commonly used file formats begin with well-known patterns (headers) and could therefore be prone to _____ attack.

G117   The attack where sender is made to generate ciphertext for a specific plaintext (chosen by the attacker) is known as _____ attack.

G118   The attack used for tricking users to disclose their username and passwords through fake pages is known as _____

G119   Unsolicited Bulk E-mails are called _____ emails.

G120   Rejection of external packets to broadcast address helps prevent _____ attack.

G121   Configuring the routers to not forward packets directed to broadcast addresses helps prevent _____ attack.

G122   Termination of the Internet connection by sending a forged TCP reset packet is known as _____

G123   In a(n) _____ attack an attacker is able to inject client-side scripts into Web pages.

G124   The attack where a client repeatedly sends SYN (synchronization) packets to every port on a server (usually) using fake IP addresses is known as _____ attack.

G125   *Half-open* attack is another name for _____ attack.

G126   Sending a series of connection requests (SYN packets) before the prior connections can time out is indication of _____ attack.

G127   The attacker sending TCP connection requests faster than the target (victim) machine can process is known as the _____ attack.

G128 In SYN flood attack, the attacker sends a series of _____ packets to the victim machine, but does not send the _____ packets to the victim, in response to the victim's _____ packets.

G129 Host A sending TCP connection requests to host B, but not responding to B's messages to complete the connection is indicative of _____ attack.

G130 Attack in which a rogue DHCP server sends forged DHCP responses to devices in a network is known as _____

G131 An effective method to shield networks from unauthenticated DHCP clients is via the use of _____ on network switches.

G132 Ensuring that DHCP servers assign IP addresses to only selected systems identified by their MAC addresses is known as

_____

G133 _____ prevents unauthorized (rogue) DHCP servers from offering IP addresses to DHCP clients.

G134 Timing attacks in public-key cryptography systems involve extensive analysis of _____ times in order to determine private key.

G135 An attacker taking control of a session between the server and a client is known as _____

G136 Changing the mapping of domain name to IP address in DNS server or DNS cache is known as _____

G137 Redirecting traffic intended for a (genuine) Web site to some other (rogue) site is achieved by changing the _____ for that Web site in _____

G138 The attack which redirects traffic intended for a (genuine) Web site to some other (rogue) site is known as _____

G139 An attack that redirects victims to a bogus website, even after correctly inputting the intended site is known as _____

G140   Email attack that is targeted toward a specific user is known as
_____

G141   Attack using a fake caller-ID posing as a trusted organization attempting to get sensitive information via the phone is known as
_____

G142   Attacks that use phishing methods through text messaging are known as _____

G143   Type of spam targeting users of instant messaging (IM) services is known as _____

G144   False information (propaganda) about an attack which is not existent is known as _____

G145   Smurfing attack is also known as _____ or
_____

G146   Process used to identify weaknesses of cryptosystems by locating patterns in the ciphertext is known as _____

G147   The worst-case time (trying all key possibilities) required to break a key of length L bits, while processing K keys per second, is _____ seconds.

G148   While processing K keys per second, the length L of a key that can be broken in a given time T (in the worst-case) is _____ bits.

G149   Preinstalled public keys of the root CAs in the client (PC/laptop) browsers defends the root-level verification against _____ attack.

G150   Use of random delays or blinding computations are countermeasures to thwart _____ attacks.

G151   A bad web site sending browser request to a good web site, using credentials of an innocent victim is known as
_____

G152   The cryptanalysis technique which attempt to deduce information from traffic patterns is known as _____

G153   The botnet (network of bots) is remotely controlled by the hacker (*bot herder*) usually through the _____ protocol.

G154   A technique used to thwart dictionary attacks on passwords is known as _____

G155   Enforcing re-authentication of users before allowing transactions to occur, mitigates _____

G156   The process wherein the response from the victim system to an attacker is deliberately delayed to the point of timing out the connection is known as _____

G157   Placing code within a web page that redirects the client's browser to attack another site upon opening the web page in client's browser is known as _____

G158   Insertion of bits in data stream with the purpose of thwarting traffic analysis is known as _____

H. Network Security

H1   The _____ is security added between the TCP and IP layers.

H2   The security mechanism most commonly used with Hypertext Transfer Protocol (HTTP) is _____

H3   Secure Sockets Layer (SSL) has now been replaced by _____

H4   The TLS handshake uses _____ encryption to establish a shared key between the two computers.

H5   The protocol which handles the echo request/reply messages for the ping command is the _____

H6   The number of encryption devices required in the link encryption with N links between a pair of hosts is _____

H7   The number of encryption devices required in the end-to-end encryption with N links between a pair of hosts is _____

H8   A packet going over N links using link encryption is encrypted/decrypted _____ times.

H9   The security protocol used for tunneling in a VPN is _____

H10   A free and open-source software which facilitates anonymous communication is _____

H11   In Tor (The onion router) the only IP address visible to the destination website is that of the _____

H12   All the traffic arriving at the destination node via a Tor network will have the source address of the _____ node.

H13   The protocol which provides the essential routing function of all packets is the _____

H14   The protocol which provides reliable processes to process communication is the _____

H15   The protocol which transmits control messages between networked devices is the _____

H16   Secure HTTP functions at the _____ layer.

H17   For gateway-to-gateway communications, IPSec runs mainly in _____ mode.

H18   For host-to-host communications, IPSec runs mainly in _____ mode.

H19   IPSec encrypts only the packet payload in _____ mode of VPN.

H20   IPSec encrypts both the packet payload and header in _____ mode.

H21   In the _____ mode of VPN, both header and body of messages are encrypted.

H22   In the _____ mode of VPN only the payload is encrypted.

H23   In the _____ mode of VPN, two remote hosts on secure (private) networks can directly establish a secure (logical) link going via a public network (Internet).

H24   In the _____ mode of VPN, individual hosts on secure (private) networks perform encryption of messages.

H25   In the _____ mode of VPN, designated server performs encryption of packets going from the secure private network to the public network (Internet).

H26   The *ping* command makes use of the _____ protocol.

H27   The command used to determine if a host is active on a network is _____

H28   In SSL, the initial vector (IV) is sent during _____

H29   SSL (Secure Sockets Layer) works between _____ and _____ (of TCP/IP protocol) layers.

H30   Agreement on the cipher schemes to be employed during the SSL session is done during _____

H31   The security services provided by SSL record protocol for messages are _____ and _____

H32   Encapsulating security payload (ESP) is a protocol used in _____

H33   Port scan to determine if a TCP port is open, sends out _____

H34   An application layer protocol that facilitates managing and monitoring the network devices is _____

H35   Remote users on private networks can communicate securely using intermediary insecure public network (ex. Internet) using _____

H36   The two types of VPNs are _____ VPNs and _____ VPNs.

H37   Site-to-site VPNs are also known as _____ VPNs.

H38   Individual users can connect to private networks at home and access resources remotely using _____ VPNs.

H39   A remote-access VPN typically depends on either _____ or _____ for secure connection over public network (Internet).

H40   Mapping of host/site names to numeric IP addresses is done by _____

H41   Reverse name lookup means fetching _____ associated with a _____

H42   The detection of hosts or devices in a network is known as _____

H43   Ping sweep is also known as _____ sweep.

H44   Technique that facilitates mapping of IP address to live hosts is known as _____

H45   _____ is a popular standardized network protocol analysis tool that allows in-depth check and analysis of packets from different protocols.

H46   A technique used by penetration testers to compromise any system within a network for targeting other systems is known as _____

H47   Checking for live systems, open ports and identification of services running on the systems are done using _____

H48   The network scanning technique used for determining which range of IP addresses map to live/running hosts is known as _____

H49   The ping sweep consists of _____ requests.

H50   SSL uses _____ for authenticating messages.

H51   IPSec (Secure Internet Protocol) makes use of _____ different protocols for securing data at the network level.

H52   The three different protocols used by IPSec are _____, _____, and _____.

H53   The protocol used for starting, preserving and terminating any real time sessions over the internet is the _____

H54   Ensuring that the traffic originating from a given domain (outbound traffic) have valid source addresses is known as _____ filtering.

H55   Blocking all outgoing packets with source IP addresses which are outside the range assigned to the network, is known as _____

H56   Blocking all incoming packets having source IP addresses assigned to computers inside the network, is known as _____

H57   The security properties provided by TLS are _____, _____, and _____

H58   In TLS, messages are encrypted using _____

H59   In TLS, message integrity is provided by the use of _____

H60   In TLS, the servers authenticate themselves to the clients by the use of _____

H61   The SSL (TLS) takes unencrypted data from the _____ layer, encrypts it and then passes it to the _____ layer.

H62   _____ provides security to data passing from transport layer (TCP) to network layer (IP).

H63   The process where two entities first exchange control packets before sending data to each other is called _____

H64   The process of gathering IP addresses of machines on the network, the operating systems on the machines, is known as _____

H65   The cryptographic parameters used between two computers using SSL or TLS are negotiated/exchanges using a series of steps known as _____

H66   The three cryptographic protections provided by SSL and TLS are _____, _____, and _____

H67   In IPSec, the secret key together with a set of cryptographic parameters is known as _____

H68   In IPSec, the attribute which specifies whether the data packet is protected by confidentiality or message integrity or both is known as _____ attribute.

H69   In IPSec, the attribute which specifies how much of the data packet is protected is known as _____ attribute.

H70   The two mode attributes (choices) of IPSec are _____ and _____

H71   Tunnel mode IPSec is commonly used in _____ VPN.

H72   Transport mode IPSec is commonly used in _____ VPN.

H73   In _____ mode, IPsec header is inserted into the IP packet.

H74   In _____ mode, entire IP packet is encrypted and becomes a payload of a new IP packet.

H75   The functionalities provided by IPsec are _____, _____, and _____

H76   The combined authentication/encryption function of IPSec is provided by _____

H77   In a VPN, prevention of unauthorized users from penetrating the virtual private network is done using _____

H78   In a VPN, prevention unauthorized users from reading messages sent over the virtual private network is done using _____

H79   In a VPN (Virtual Private Network), the mechanism of sending a packet through a public network between private networks is known as _____

H80   *IPSec* provides security at the _____ layer.

H81   *TLS* provides security at the _____ layer.

H82   *SSL* (Secure Socket Layer) provides security at the _____ layer.

H83   *PGP* provides security at the _____ layer.

H84   The number of times the body of the packet is encrypted + decrypted when sent from a host A to a host B via N links using end-to-end encryption is _____

H85   A packet with the correct checksum, but failing the integrity check is rejected by the _____ at the receiver.

H86   Given M hosts communicating over a network path with N links, the number of encryption devices required in the combined link and end-to-end encryption is _____

H87   The packets of a message sent from a host A to a host B over N links using link encryption is encrypted _____ times.

H88   The packets of a message sent from a host A to a host B over N links using combined end-to-end and link encryption is encrypted _____ times.

H89   The number of times a message (packet) is encrypted going from host A to a host B via N links with end-to-end encryption is _____

H90   The number of times the header of packet is encrypted going from host A to a host B via N links with link encryption is _____

H91   Given that the header of a packet is encrypted 18 times going from host A to a host B using link encryption, the number of intermediary links between A and B, is _____

H92   Given that a packet (header/body) going from host A to a host B using combined link and end-to-end encryption is subjected to a total of 18 encryptions/decryptions, the number of intermediary links between A and B, is _____

H93   Multiple systems can share a single IP address using a service known as _____

H94   A standard protocol for transmitting and receiving files from client to server through a network is the _____

H95   A port number is always associated with _____ of the host and the _____

H96   The port number of File Transfer Protocol (FTP) for data transfer is ____

H97   The port number of File Transfer Protocol (FTP) is for control signals is ___

H98   The port number of Secure Shell (SSH) which is used for secure login is ___

H99   The port number of Telnet which is used for remote login service is ___

H100   The port number of Simple Mail Transfer Protocol (SMTP) E-mail routing is ___

H101   The port number of Domain Name System (DNS) service is ___

H102   The port number of Dynamic Host Configuration Protocol (DHCP) is ___

H103   The port number of Hypertext Transfer Protocol (HTTP) is ___

H104   The Port number of Kerberos service is ___

H105   The port number of Post Office Protocol (POP3) is ___

H106   The port number of Network News Transfer Protocol (NNTP) is

___

H107   The port number of Network Time Protocol (NTP) is ___

H108   The port number of Internet Message Access Protocol (IMAP) is

___

H109   The port number(s) of Simple Network Management Protocol (SNMP) is(are) ___

H110   The port number of Internet Relay Chat (IRC) is ___

H111   The port number of HTTPS (HTTP Secure – HTTP over TLS/SSL) is ___

H112   Bridges work at the ___ layer.

H113   Routers work at the ___ layer.

H114   The host (or device or software) that connects two different environments is known as ___

H115   ICMP works at the _____ layer.

H116   _____ enables a LAN to use one set of IP addresses for internal traffic and another set of addresses for external traffic.

H117   A signaling protocol widely used for VoIP communications sessions is the _____

H118   Ensuring that valid source addresses are used in all packets can be (fairly) easily done at the _____

H119   TCP and UDP port scanning is carried out at the _____ layer.

H120   ICMP scanning is carried out at the _____ layer.

H121   FTPS (FTP Secure) is an extension of the file transfer protocol (FTP) that adds security via the use of _____

H122   The protocol used for monitoring the health of network equipment, computers, and devices is the

_____

H123   IP protocol is a connectionless protocol that deals with the _____ and _____ of packets.

H124   The protocol which assigns dynamic IP addresses to hosts (on power-up) is _____

H125   The routing where a packet goes through a network on a predetermined path is known as _____

H126   _____ is a set of extensions to DNS which provides cryptographic authentication of DNS data to DNS clients.

H127   The SSL _____ protocol is layered on top of SSL _____ protocol.

H128   The _____ and _____ segments are needed to begin a TCP connection.

H129   TLS uses _____ cryptography for authenticating the identity of the communicating parties.

H130   Upon receiving a SYN packet, a port on a remote host that is open for incoming connection requests, will respond with a _____ packet.

H131   Upon receiving a SYN packet, a port on a remote host that is closed for incoming connection requests, will respond with a(n) _____ packet.

H132   Record in DNS containing the Internet email route is called _____ record.

H133   The protocol which does the translation of IP address to MAC (media access control) address is the _____

H134   ARP (Address Resolution Protocol) poisoning affects the translation of _____ to _____

H135   The unique ____ bit identifier assigned to a network card (network interface controller-NIC) is called _____

H136   The most common way of providing secure connection to remote users over an insecure network (ex. Internet) is via _____

H137   Encapsulating Security Payload (ESP) part of the IPSec protocol suite, is primarily designed to provide _____

H138   The standards-based version of Secure Sockets Layer (SSL) version 3 is known as _____

H139   Security controls at the _____ layer can be used to protect the data in a single communication session between two hosts.

H140   Address Resolution Protocol (ARP) reply contains the correct mapping between _____ and _____ addresses.

H141   An intermediate LAN that is between two screening routers (or firewalls) of a network is known as _____

H142 The network of essential servers (ex. Web server, email server) placed between a private (trusted) network and the Internet (public network), is known as _____

H143 Encapsulating packets of an internal (private) network protocol into a packet of an external network protocol (typically the Internet) and transmitting is known as _____

H144 The IPSec protocol responsible for creation and maintenance of security associations between communicating devices is the

_____

H145 The authentication header (AH) of IPSec provides _____ and _____ of messages.

H146 The encapsulating security protection (ESP) of IPSec provides _____, _____, and _____ of messages.

H147 The port that should be blocked when it has been determined that an intruder has been using Telnet for unauthorized access is ____

H148 The port(s) that should be blocked when it has been determined that an intruder has been using SNMP for unauthorized access is/are _____

H149 An established connection without specifying a username or password is known as _____

H150 Information about which key is being used with a packet (key-to-packet mapping) is known as _____

H151 The protocol used for network diagnostics and performance is

_____

H152 The maximum size of a block transported by SSL record protocol is _____

H153 A software utility that scans a single machine or a range of IP addresses checking for a response on service connections is known as _____

H154 _____ is a software utility that scans a range of IP addresses checking for known weaknesses in software configuration and accessible services.

H155 A software utility that is used to analyze network communications is known as _____

H156 A software utility that compiles a list of all systems, devices, and network hardware present within a network segment is known as

_____

H157 _____ is an assessment tool for checking particular versions and patch levels of a service.

H158 _____ is an assessment tool that reports information used to identify single points of failure.

H159 Protocol analyzer is also often referred to as _____

H160 Routing where the sender of a packet can partially or completely specify the route the packet takes through the network is known as _____

H161 The most commonly used message authentication code (MAC) used in IPSec is _____

H162 The technical controls that track activity within a network, on a network device, or on a computer are known as _____

H163 The routing tables at the routers are based on _____ addresses.

H164 The protocol for accessing and maintaining distributed directory information services in a network using Internet Protocol (IP) is the _____

H165 Message security being maintained, despite being sent over insecure channel, is known as _____

H166 Under channel security, message security relies on protocols below the _____ layer to handle the encryption.

H167   The process of trying to list all servers in a network is known as
_____

I. Web Security and Application Security

I1   _____ is another widely used Email security system other than PGP.

I2   The private–public key pairs of a user in PGP are stored in the _____ key ring.

I3   To make it compatible with many Email systems, PGP performs _____

I4   The number of key rings maintained by PGP is ____

I5   The session key in PGP is encrypted using the recipient's _____ key.

I6   Typically the _____ is used as the user ID in the private key ring of PGP.

I7   The number of bits used to index the Radix-64 conversion table of PGP is ____

I8   The portion of the World Wide Web that a common (popular) search engine cannot search is known as the _____

I9   The portion of the Web that is indexed by common (popular) search engine(s) is known as _____

I10   In the first instance, a cookie is sent from a _____ to a _____

I11   The portion of the Web that is accessible only via onion routing is known as_____

I12   The cookie that exists only in temporary memory while the user navigates the website is known as _____

I13   The cookie that still exists even after a user has finished navigation of the Web site is known as _____

I14   A cookie that can only be transmitted over an encrypted connection (https) is known as _____

I15   One way of not revealing the IP address of a computer (client) to any Web server is to use a(n) _____ that sits between the client and the Internet.

I16   Cookies that are sent only over HTTPS connection are known as

_____

I17   A cookie is just a data file containing the 'state' of interaction between the _____ and _____

I18   A cookie that is stored only in memory but not in a file is known as a _____

I19   Software installed on a system that is designed to intercept all traffic between the local web browser and the web server is known as _____

I20   Secure key exchange between the Web server and Web browser id provided by _____

I21   The scheme used for message encryption in current versions of S/MIME is _____

I22   In S/MIME, the ElGamal public key scheme (by default) is used to encrypt _____

I23   The default algorithms used for signing S/MIME messages are the _____ and the _____

I24   The SET (Secure Electronic Transaction) provides security at the _____ layer of the network.

I25   In SET, the session key K_S used to encrypt the payment information is itself encrypted using the _____

I26   The _____ vulnerability can be mitigated by preventing the use of HTML tags.

I27   In the e-commerce transactions between a user and business using only one-way authentication, _____ needs to authenticate _____

I28   Pretty Good Privacy (PGP) is used in _____ application.

I29   Cookies that are created by domains other than the one a user is visiting directly, are known as _____

I30   Certificates commonly used in Web applications for secure client-server communication are _____

I31   The _____ cookies are deleted when the browser is exited.

I32   A single machine serving many web sites (by having many hostnames corresponding to a single IP address) is known as _____

I33   A mail server can look up the IP of an incoming mail connection and reject it if it is listed in the _____

I34   The return addresses in the headers of all packets leaving a private network (intranet) using a proxy server are changed to the address of the _____

I35   In onion routing, all servers (except the origin and destination) via which packets are sent are _____

I36   Input validation is done at the client before it is sent to the server to process is known as _____

I37   Both HTTP and HTTPS content downloaded to browser while displaying in the same page is known as _____

I38   An XML-based language for the exchange of security information among online business partners is _____

I39   In encrypted email systems, raw 8-bit binary stream is converted to a stream of printable ASCII characters using _____

I40   Validation of values received by a server application to be within permissible limits, before processing them, is known as

_____

I41   The technology that allows web developers to reuse content by inserting the same content into multiple web documents is known as _____

I42   A decoy system that is designed to lure a potential attacker away from a critical system is known as _____

I43   A _____ delivers suspected SPAM messages with more delays.

I44   In PGP, the integrity of the message is ensured by the use of

_____

I45   While using an anonymizing proxy server, the traffic between a user and the proxy will be encrypted by using _____

I46   Rejection of email from specific IP addresses is facilitated by

_____

J. Firewalls and Intrusion Detection

J1   The simplest among the types of firewalls is the
     _____ firewall.

J2   Firewall installed on a single computer to prevent intrusion is
     known as _____ firewall.

J3   Packet filtering firewalls are implemented in the _____
     layer.

J4   The table containing rules for firewall system to provide/deny
     entry to packets is called _____

J5   Packet filtering firewalls determine the validity of every packet by
     checking against the rules defined in the _____

J6   A packet filtering firewall makes decision about allowing or
     dropping a packet based on the rules defined in the

     _____

J7   A computer (system) which acts as a relay for application-level
     traffic between two remote hosts is known as

     _____

J8   Stateful Multilayer Inspection firewalls are a combination of
     (other three types of) _____, _____, and
     _____ firewalls.

J9   The firewall with built in algorithms and complex security modes
     is the _____ firewall.

J10 The firewall incorporating multiple characteristics of different
     firewalls is the _____ firewall.

J11 Software running on a single host that restricts incoming and
     outgoing network activity for that host only is known as
     _____ firewall.

J12   A device deployed between networks to restrict the types of traffic that can pass from one network to another is known as _____

J13   The default _____ policy of a firewall is comparatively more restrictive.

J14   Firewalls that use the contents of packets together with information about other packets and connections are known as _____ firewalls.

J15   Spoofed IP packets can be prevented from leaving a network by packet filter firewall by examining the _____ of the packet.

J16   The first firewall faced by traffic coming from the Internet to an internal (protected) network is known as _____

J17   The firewall closest to the internal network of hosts is known as _____

J18   A firewall placed at the perimeter of the network as the sole link between the network and the outside world is known as _____

J19   The rule which protects the firewall from attacks is known as _____ rule.

J20   Allowing all connections except explicitly specified connections is known as _____

J21   Disallowing all connections except explicitly specified connections is known as _____

J22   A _____ firewall analyzes packets independently, without regard to other packets.

J23   Statistical filtering is also known as _____

J24   _____ firewalls protect the network for specific application layer protocol.

J25   The   filtering   rules   of   packet   filters   are   set   by
_____

J26   The primary defenses against network mapping are _____
and _____

J27   Servers that act as intermediaries between the public network and
private servers are known as _____

J28   The firewall which in addition to examining each packet, also uses
data derived from several previous packets is known as
_____ firewall.

J29   Application-level gateways are also known as _____

J30   The firewall where each incoming packet is examined, and
allowing only the ones matching the set of criteria is called
_____ firewall.

J31   Application level gateway is also known as _____ -
firewall.

J32   In a *stateless* firewall the criteria for deciding to pass or discard
the   packet   are   (1)   _____   and   (2)   the
_____

J33   Routers acting as firewalls process packets at the _____
layer.

J34   A _____ monitors traffic at selected points on a
network.

J35   A network-based IDS primarily performs _____ and
_____ to identify suspicious activity.

J36   Part of the IDS that is responsible for collecting data is known as
_____

J37   Part of the IDS that receives input from one or more sensors and
determines if an intrusion has occurred is known as _____

J38   A sensor of an IDS through which the actual traffic passes is known as _____

J39   In the context of IDS, authorized users identified as intruders are known as _____

J40   In the context of IDS, intruders not identified as intruders are known as _____

J41   In the context of IDS, the ratio of detected attacks to total attacks is known as _____

J42   The _____ IDS (Intrusion Detection System) looks for deviations from the model of accepted behavior.

J43   Nonintrusive activities misclassified as attacks are known as _____

J44   Malicious activities which fail to be identified and pass through as genuine activities are known as _____

J45   The _____ intrusion detection system monitors user and network behavior.

J46   Intrusion Prevention System (IPS) that monitors the characteristics and the events occurring within a single host is known as _____

J47   _____ intrusion detection is only effective in detecting known attacks.

J48   _____ intrusion detection is effective in detecting novel (previously unknown) attacks.

J49   Monitoring the activities and the events within a single host for suspicious activities is done by _____ IDS.

J50   Defining and using a set of rules or attack patterns to decide if a given behavior is that of an intruder in done in _____ detection.

IOIOIOIOIOIOIOIOIOIOIOIOIOIOIOIOIOIOIOIOIOIOIOIOIOIOIOIOIOIOI

Answers

(True/False)

A. Overview

A1   A threat will always cause damage to the computer/information system. *False*

A2   Prevention of attacks is easy. *False*

A3   It is impossible to prevent all kinds of attacks. *True*

A4   Traffic analysis is an active threat. *False*

A5   All attacks result in loss of data/information. *False*

A6   Diskless workstations (with no hard disk and no full operating system) are not vulnerable to viruses. *False*

A7   Auditing tools can allow or deny access to a network or computer. *False*

A8   It is impossible to reproduce data streams based on the intercepts of electromagnetic emissions radiated from a computer. *False*

A9   Integrity of data is not one of the concerns of cryptography. *False*

A10   Validation of data is one of the concerns of cryptography. *False*

A11   Hardware authentication is done in some systems by a specially designed chip which stores RSA encryption keys of the host system. *True*

A12   Security vulnerabilities are not present in the processor hardware. *False*

A13   The BIOS (Basic Input/Output System) cannot ask for a password at the start of the system. *False*

A14   Message confidentiality always implies message integrity. *False*

A15   Biometric devices cannot ensure exact matches. *True*

A16   Use of biometric devices for authentication cannot have false negatives. *__False__*

A17   Forgeries are impossible in biometric authentication systems. *__False__*

A18   The *Bell-LaPadula* model addresses data integrity issues. *__False__*

A19   The *Biba* model addresses data confidentiality issues. *__False__*

A20   The *Clark-Wilson* model addresses data integrity issues. *__True__*

B. Cryptography

B1   The algorithms used in encryption systems are usually published (publicly known). ***True***

B2   One-time pads are provably secure (unbreakable). ***True***

B3   One-time pads are commonly used in practice. ***False***

B4   The one–time pad is not practical for implementation. ***True***

B5   When all messages are distinct, but are of the same length, then it is secure to re-use the same one-time-pad for encryption. ***False***

B6   One-time pad is well suited for long messages. ***False***

B7   The diffusion property increases the difficulty of uncovering the key from the ciphertext. ***False***

B8   In any cryptosystem, some information in the plaintext will be lost upon encryption. ***False***

B9   In symmetric key encryption, confidentiality of the message lies in the secrecy of the algorithm. ***False***

B10   It is never the case that two different keys generate the same ciphertext for the same message. ***False***

B11   Symmetric key system cannot support nonrepudiation without employing a trusted third party. ***True***

B12   Stream (mode) cypher is better suited to encrypting files, emails, and databases. ***False***

B13   Stream ciphers usually operate slower than block ciphers. ***False***

B14   The unit of encryption in stream ciphers is usually small (Byte/Bit). ***True***

B15   Stream ciphers are used in file transfers and emails. ***False***

B16   Block ciphers are used in short data transfers between Web servers and browsers. *False*

B17   The commonly used defense against brute force attack is using a larger key. *True*

B18   The efficiency (computation time) of encryption/decryption is independent of the key size. *False*

B19   A stream cipher can work on bits of data (one bit at a time). *True*

B20   A stream cipher will not work on data more than a byte in size. *False*

B21   Software implementation of stream ciphers is faster than those of block ciphers. *False*

B22   The Data Encryption Standard (DES) uses several intricate and complex functions during the encryption process. *False*

B23   In DES, the decryption algorithm is identical to the encryption algorithm. *True*

B24   All rounds in DES are identical. *True*

B25   DES has been broken due to flaws in its algorithm. *False*

B26   A row of an S-box in DES may contain duplicate elements. *False*

B27   No two elements in any row of an S-box of DES are the same. *True*

B28   No two elements in any column of an S-box of DES are the same. *False*

B29   No two S-boxes of DES give the same output for the same row and column numbers. *False*

B30   3DES can be used to decrypt data which has been encrypted with DES. *True*

B31   The underlying encryption algorithm in 3DES is different than in DES. *__False__*

B32   3DES requires three times as many calculations as DES. *__True__*

B33   3DES has three times the security of DES. *__False__*

B34   In DES encryption, the original key is never used for encryption in any of the rounds. *__True__*

B35   DES is considered weak due to known flaws in its cryptographic algorithm. *__False__*

B36   DES is now considered weak due to its small key size. *__True__*

B37   The CFB (Cipher Feed Back) mode of DES gives the effect of stream cipher. *__True__*

B38   In the ECB (Electronic Code Book) mode of DES, an error in one cipher-text block propagates to other plaintext-blocks. *__False__*

B39   In the CBC (Cipher Block Chaining) mode of DES, a bit error in plaintext block P_1 affects all the cipher-text blocks. *__True__*

B40   In the ECB mode of DES, the same plaintext block produces the same ciphertext block. *__True__*

B41   In the ECB (Electronic Code Book) mode of DES, the decryption of any block of ciphertext the C_i is independent on any other ciphertext block(s). *__True__*

B42   The ciphertext produced by ECB mode for lengthy messages exhibits regularities corresponding to those in the plaintext. *__True__*

B43   The AES supports different key lengths. *__True__*

B44   AES supports plaintext blocks of different lengths. *__False__*

B45   All rounds of the AES are identical. *__False__*

B46   In AES, the decryption algorithm makes use of the expanded key in reverse order. *__True__*

B47   In AES, the decryption algorithm is identical to the encryption algorithm. **_False_**

B48   In the Mix Column transformation of AES, each byte of a column is mapped to a new value that is a function of all four bytes of that column. **_True_**

B49   In the S-Box of AES, all entries are distinct. **_True_**

B50   In the Inverse S-Box of AES, not all entries are distinct. **_False_**

B51   The ranges of values in the S-Box and Inverse S-Box of AES are not the same. **_False_**

B52   AES is a byte-oriented cipher (all operations are purely byte-level). **_True_**

B53   In AES encryption, the original key is never used for encryption in any of the rounds. **_True_**

B54   In Advanced Encryption Standard (AES), the 'shift rows' step contributes to confusion. **_False_**

B55   RC4 is an example of a block cipher. **_False_**

B56   RC4 is used in SSL (Secure Socket Layer) and TLS (Transport Layer Security). **_True_**

B57   Public key encryption is much slower than symmetric key encryption. **_True_**

B58   Public key encryption is widely used for encryption of data. **_False_**

B59   Public-key system is commonly used in the distribution of secret (symmetric) keys. **_True_**

B60   In Public-key encryption, message can be encrypted using any key in the pair and decrypted with the other. **_True_**

B61   The public key system cannot be used for both confidentiality and authentication at the same time. **_False_**

B62   RSA encryption works on blocks of input data. ***True***

B63   RSA cannot be used for (generating) digital signatures. ***False***

B64   RSA can be used for distributing symmetric keys. ***True***

B65   In the RSA key pairs {*e*, *n*} and {*d*, *n*}, *n* (which is the product of two large primes) is publicly known. ***True***

B66   In the RSA key pairs {*e*, *n*} and {*d*, *n*}, *n* (which is the product of two large primes) is kept secret. ***False***

B67   The Diffie–Hellman scheme provides public key encryption of messages. ***False***

B68   The conventional encryption itself could serve the purpose of authentication (in some cases). ***True***

B69   Encryption using the private key of a user does not provide confidentiality. ***True***

B70   Public key encryption is computationally more expensive compared to symmetric key encryption (for similar sized plaintext). ***True***

B71   Encryption using the public key of sender provides authentication. ***False***

B72   In public-key cryptography, encrypting the message using sender's private key provides confidentiality. ***False***

B73   In public-key cryptography, encrypting the message using receiver's public key provides confidentiality. ***True***

B74   In public-key cryptography, encrypting the message using sender's private key provides authentication. ***True***

B75   Elliptic Curve Cryptography (ECC) is a public key technique. ***True***

B76   The key size of Elliptic Curve Cryptography (ECC) is about the same as that of RSA (for the same security strength). ***False***

B77   Elliptic Curve Cryptography (ECC) can be used to compute digital signatures. *True*

B78   Elliptic Curve Cryptography (ECC) cannot be used for distribution of symmetric keys. *False*

B79   *All* cryptanalysis techniques attempt to deduce information based only on message content. *False*

B80   The Diffie-Hellman scheme can be used to compute digital signatures. *False*

B81   The Diffie-Hellman scheme is not prone to man-in-the-middle attack. *False*

B82   The Diffie-Hellman scheme is used for encryption of symmetric keys. *False*

B83   The Diffie-Hellman scheme is a public-key method for encrypting data. *False*

B84   Diffie-Hellman scheme is a method for secure exchange of public keys. *False*

B85   In a public-key system, the private key of a user is also known to the certification authority. *False*

B86   In most public key cryptosystems, the encryption algorithms are kept secret. *False*

B87   Nonrepudiation can be ensured in symmetric key systems without a trusted third party. *False*

B88   There is no need for a trusted third party to ensure nonrepudiation in a public-key system. *True*

C. Key Generation, Distribution, and Management

C1   A session key is a symmetric key that is used just once. ***True***

C2   A session key is (usually) never a private-public key pair. ***True***

C3   The cryptographic keys may not be stored in a separate physical device (ex. smartcard) rather than in the computer. ***False***

C4   In all of the public-key key distribution protocols, there is no need of a central agent. ***False***

C5   Public-key key distribution protocols are much simpler than those used in symmetric key distribution. ***False***

C6   It is never the case that two certification authorities (CAs) issue certificates for each other. ***False***

C7   Session keys require generation of pseudorandom numbers. ***True***

C8   Key exchange and authentication protocols are usually combined in practice. ***True***

C9   Key exchange protocols are based on public key methods only. ***False***

C10   Upon compromise of the private key of a web server, the key is revoked. ***True***

C11   Session keys (which are used for short durations) are usually asymmetric keys. ***False***

C12   Distribution of the keys is a major problem (impractical) with the use of one-time pads. ***True***

C13   The distribution of symmetric shared key among the communicating entities is a non-trivial task. ***True***

C14   A single KDC can work well for large networks. ***False***

147

C15   Public key system eases the task of symmetric shared key distribution among the communicating entities. ***True***

C16   Public-key cryptography is more commonly used for the distribution of symmetric keys among communicating entities, than for encryption. ***True***

C17   Public-key encryption is often used in the secure sharing of one-time symmetric session key. ***True***

C18   Public-key (asymmetric key) encryption is more commonly used for encryption of keys used in symmetric key encryption rather than data. ***True***

C19   RSA Tokens can be used multiple times during access control. ***False***

C20   The keys stored in the Trusted Platform Module (TPM) chip cannot be read by software. ***True***

C21   Random numbers are used in the generation of (temporary) session keys. ***True***

C22   Plaintext public key is susceptible to man-in-the-middle attack. ***True***

D. Authentication, Hash Functions, Digital Signatures / Certificates

D1   The size of the MAC (Message Authentication Code) depends on the size of the message. *False*

D2   It is impossible for two different messages to have the same MAC (using the same function). *False*

D3   The computation of Hash code (Message digest) requires a secret key. *False*

D4   No two distinct messages can have the same message digest. *False*

D5   In a good Hash function, the hash code is a function of all the bits of the message. *True*

D6   It is possible for two different messages to have the same message digest. *True*

D7   The Hash functions are irreversible. *True*

D8   The Message digest serves as a check of message integrity. *True*

D9   The Message Authentication Code (MAC) is generated using irreversible functions. *True*

D10   The original message can be reconstructed from the Message Authentication Code (MAC). *False*

D11   The Message Authentication Code (MAC) serves as a check of message integrity. *True*

D12   Public-key system is also used in the distribution of secret (symmetric) keys. *True*

D13   A single KDC (Key Distribution Center) can work well for large networks. *False*

D14   Hash functions make use of a key for the generation of the hash value.

D15   The Message Authentication Code is of variable length. *False*

D16   Message authentication can be achieved by the use of Hash function. *True*

D17   The computation of Hash code (Message digest) requires a secret key. *False*

D18   Hash functions do not require a key for the generation of the message digest (hash value). *True*

D19   In several applications, the message is not encrypted, but sent in plaintext with associated MAC. *True*

D20   The hash values of two different inputs using the same hash function *H* can never be the same. *False*

D21   The Hash function is a *one–way* function. *True*

D22   A Message Authentication Code is not part of a Kerberos authentication implementation. *True*

D23   Kerberos uses a trusted third-party scheme for the authentication service. *True*

D24   Kerberos is an example of a single sign-on system. *True*

D25   Kerberos uses symmetric key cryptography. *True*

D26   Kerberos does not provide end-to-end security. *False*

D27   Kerberos uses symmetric key cryptography to encrypt messages. *True*

D28   Kerberos provides access, authentication, and authorization. *True*

D29   Session keys never reside on the users' workstations under Kerberos. *False*

D30   Shared secret keys are never stored on the users' workstations under Kerberos. *__False__*

D31   Kerberos essentially provides a trusted third-party authentication service. *__True__*

D32   In Kerberos the authentication of servers to clients is optional. *__True__*

D33   In Kerberos the authentication of clients to servers is optional. *__False__*

D34   Kerberos does not detect password-guessing attacks. *__True__*

D35   The *remote authentication dial-in user service* (*RADIUS*) network protocol provides client/server authentication and authorization, but not audits of remote users. *__False__*

D36   *RADIUS* encrypts all traffic between the client and the server. *__False__*

D37   There are applications which require message authentication, but not message confidentiality. *__True__*

D38   Message authentication is required for encrypted messages only. *__False__*

D39   Message authentication can only be done using public-key techniques. *__False__*

D40   In keyed hash MAC two communicating parties share a common secret key. *__True__*

D41   Although keyed hash MAC uses a common secret key, there is no encryption/decryption in any of the steps. *__True__*

D42   HMAC uses asymmetric encryption. *__False__*

D43   Digital signatures are more efficient than MACs for authentication. *__False__*

D44   Digital signatures are not used for confidentiality. *__True__*

D45 A message digest provides data integrity in addition to authentication. *True*

D46 Secure hash functions are not subject to attacks. *False*

D47 The collision resistance property of any (well known) secure hash function has never been violated. *False* [MD5's vulnerability has been shown]

D48 Use of public key certificates prevents man-in-the-middle attacks. *True*

D49 The root certification authority (CA) cannot be an issuing certification authority. *False*

D50 The certification authority (CA) can generate the private key corresponding to the public key of the digital certificate that it generates. *False*

D51 The root certification authority's certificate is always self-signed. *True*

D52 The root certificates of all well-known CAs must be kept by the browsers. *True*

D53 During the validation of the digital certificate of a user, all signatures in the chain of trust need not be verified. *False*

D54 The same set of classes for different types of digital certificates are used by the different certification authorities (CA). *False*

D55 The longer message digest has lesser chance of collisions. *True*

D56 Given the hash value of the message, the original message can be easily recovered if the Hash function is known. *False*

D57 In a MAC-based authentication scheme, the communicating parties should establish a shared key. *True*

D58 There exist hash functions which do not make use of secret keys. *True*

D59   Message authentication code (MAC) is not a key component of Kerberos. *True*

D60   Digital signatures are not susceptible to birthday attacks. *False*

D61   A user sending the same message to multiple recipients must use a different digital signature for each recipient for authentication. *False*

D62   Digital signatures require an underlying Public Key Infrastructure (PKI) with certification authorities. *True*

D63   Public-key encryption is used for creating a message authentication code (MAC). *False*

D64   When using a message authentication code (MAC), the communicating entities need to have a shared secret key. *True*

D65   The algorithm/formula for computing the message authentic code (MAC) is kept secret. *False*

D66   The Diffie-Hellman method does not provide authentication. *True*

D67   Signing the original message is seldom done in practice. *True*

D68   The size of message digest is dependent of the size of the message. *False*

D69   Original messages can never be reconstructed from message digests. *True*

D70   Use of message digests helps in detecting attacks on message integrity. *True*

D71   All message digests are generated with the use of secret keys. *False*

D72   The algorithms used in the generation of message authentication codes (MACs) are kept secret. *False*

D73   The hash functions used in the generation of message digests (ex. MD5) are publicly known. *True*

D74 The (once popular) MD5 Hash function has no known vulnerabilities. *False*

D75 The Digital Signature Algorithm used in the Digital Signature Standard (DSS) cannot be used for encryption. *True*

D76 The Digital Signature Algorithm used in the Digital Signature Standard (DSS) can be used for key exchange. *False*

D77 A message must be encrypted before being digitally signed. *False*

D78 Generation of a digital signature requires the public key of the receiver. *False*

D79 Serial numbers associated with certificates issued by a CA are unique. *True*

D80 Just the serial number is not sufficient to uniquely identify a certificate within a CA. *False*

D81 DSS is used for encryption of keys in symmetric key cryptosystems. *False*

D82 DSS is used for symmetric key distribution. *False*

D83 DSS cannot be used for key exchange. *True*

D84 DSS can be used for encryption. *False*

D85 Digital signature provides confidentiality of messages. *False*

D86 The private-public key pair is generated and assigned by the certification authority (CA). *False*

D87 A cryptographic hash function produces different outputs at different times for the same input. *False*

D88 Computing the hash using SHA-1 requires a correct secret key. *False*

D89 Digital signatures use public-key cryptography to provide both integrity and authentication. *True*

D90   Hash functions (ex. SHA-1) does not use a secret key in computing the hash. ***True***

D91   The strength of a hash function against brute-force attacks is independent length of the hash code produced by the hash algorithm. ***False***

D92   Computing SHA-1 hash for a data item requires a correct secret key. ***False***

D93   A secure hash function will never produce any collisions. ***False***

D94   Digital signatures prevent the forgery of the messages by the recipients. ***True***

D95   MAC (message authentication code) provides both confidentiality and integrity. ***False***

D96   The secret key used for message encryption and the secret key used for generating the message authentication code (MAC) are usually the same. ***False***

D97   Typically, the hashed form of the passwords are stored on a server. ***True***

D98   Since the passwords are hashed, it is impossible for a malicious entity in possession of the password file to gain access to a system. ***False***

D99   Encryption of password that is sent across a network to log on to a remote system is not vulnerable to eavesdropping attack. ***False***

D100   Use of salt effectively increases the length of the password. ***True***
D101   The rainbow table is a list of passwords. ***False***

D102   The rainbow table is a list of hashes of passwords. ***True***

D103   Password cracking using large rainbow tables can be made more difficult by using larger salt values. ***True***

D104   The length of the hash of password and salt has no effect in making password cracking more difficult. ***False***

D105 Use of random numbers in the authentication process defends against replay attacks. **_True_**

D106 A virtual password is derived from a passphrase. **_True_**

D107 A certificate authority that issues a TLS certificate to a site can decrypt TLS traffic to that site. **_False_**

D108 The certification authority has access to the private keys of the users. **_False_**

E. Software and Operating Systems Security

E1 Using buffer overflow vulnerability, an attacker can place malicious code in memory. *True*

E2 Validating all input is one of the means of preventing incomplete mediation. *True*

E3 Time–of–check to Time–of–use errors would not happen if there is no gap in time between a check and the corresponding operation. *True*

E4 Undocumented access points in the programs are inserted by the attacker. *False*

E5 A normally null–terminated string which is unterminated will not be a vulnerability. *False*

E6 Even in a single user system (ex. laptop), the OS should enforce memory protection mechanisms. *True*

E7 A fence register can be used for relocation of a user's program. *True*

E8 Access control list contains one list per object containing subjects and access rights. *True*

E9 Two users having shared access to a segment must have the same access rights. *False*

E10 The default set of access rights is always recommended to be the rule of least privilege. *True*

E11 Poorly written programs (ex. buffer overflows) could be causes of security vulnerabilities. *True*

E12 The operating system access controls comprise administrative controls. *False*

E13 The reference monitor mediates only a subset of accesses between subjects and objects. *False*

E14 The reference monitor is called upon for every access attempt. *True*

E15 Virtual machines cannot be used to provide secure, isolated sandboxes for running untrusted applications. *False*

E16 Virtualization can be used to simulate networks of independent computers. *True*

E17 Maintenance hooks inserted in applications for quick maintenance will not pose serious security risks. *False*

E18 Preventing authorized users from making improper modifications to data is not a goal of data integrity. *False*

E19 Fuzzing can typically expose buffer overflows. *True*

E20 Fuzzing cannot typically expose SQL injection vulnerabilities. *False*

E21 Fuzzing can typically expose missing authentication/authorization checks. *False*

E22 Buffer overflow vulnerability can be exploited in CGI scripts. *True*

E23 Buffer overflow vulnerability can be exploited in the Lightweight Directory Access Protocol (LDAP). *True*

E24 Validating data input is not an effective method to mitigate buffer overflows. *False*

E25 Validating data input is an effective method to mitigate cross-site scripting attacks. *True*

E26 Fuzzing cannot allow an attacker to identify vulnerabilities within a closed source software application. *False*

E27 A stack overflow vulnerability cannot be used for any form of denial-of-service attack. *False*

E28 A buffer overflow could lead to corruption of data. *True*

E29 A buffer overflow could lead to memory access violation. *True*

E30 A buffer overflow cannot be exploited to force unexpected transfer of control in a program. *False*

E31 A buffer is located only in the stack area, but not in the heap area. *False*

E32 Many computer security vulnerabilities can be traced back to poor programming practices. *True*

E33 It is not possible for a system to be compromised during the installation process. *False*

E34 It is possible for malware to get into a system during the installation process. *True*

E35 Certain bugs in programs will cause security vulnerabilities. *True*

E36 All bugs in programs may not be security vulnerabilities. *True*

E37 Large software systems cannot be guaranteed to be bug free. *True*

E38 Configuration of the operating system has no effect on system vulnerabilities. *False*

E39 Default configurations of operating systems are more vulnerable to attacks. *True*

E40 Execution of arbitrary code at a privileged level cannot happen as a result buffer overflow. *False*

E41 Mobile code is software that is executed on mobile devices. *False*

E42 Compliance test (that tests the security measures in place) is a non-malicious attack against a network. *False*

E43   Despite memory protection of a typical operating system, malicious code running in kernel mode can write to memory areas of applications. *True*

E44   Buffer overflows are possible in every high-level language. *False*

E45   It is impossible to prevent buffer overflows when the programming language does not provide safeguards for buffer overflows to happen. *False*

E46   Some programming languages facilitate detection of buffer overflow problems at compile time. *True*

E47   Buffer overflow attacks target only buffers located in the stack, but not in the data section of a process. *False*

E48   There exist run-time defenses that provide some protection for already existing buffer overflow vulnerabilities in programs. *True*

E49   Software developed using defensive (secure) programming never fails. *False*

E50   Software developed using defensive (secure) programming does not usually crash abruptly upon encountering an error. *True*

E51   Certain attacks can cause erroneous conditions in a running program. *True*

E52   Eliminating buffer overflow problem would completely eliminate the problem of Internet worms. *False*

E53   Eliminating buffer overflow problem would not completely eliminate the problem of botnets. *True*

E54   A system configuration change has no effect on disabling a vulnerable service. *False*

E55   Access control lists cannot represent everything that an access control matrices can represent. *False*

E56   The Access Control List (ACL) rules are based on address, protocols and packet attributes. *True*

E57   Network administrators cannot create their own ACL rules. ***False***

E58   *Security assessment* tests the security measures in place in a network. ***False***

E59   Log files related to security events are usually stored on the local machine. ***False***

E60   The log files related to security events are seldom stored on the intranet. ***True***

E61   The log files related to security events are usually stored on an offline storage. ***True***

E62   Penetration testing includes all of the vulnerability assessment processes. ***True***

E63   Penetration testing weakens the network's security level. ***False***

F. Malware

F1   Worm needs a host program to propagate. *False*

F2   Worms do not need a host program for their replication. *True*

F3   All viruses cause destruction of programs and/or data. *False*

F4   Viruses cannot replicate on their own. *True*

F5   Rootkits can *only* reside at the user level of an operating system. *False*

F6   Rootkits cannot reside at the kernel level of an operating system. *False*

F7   Rootkits could reside in firmware. *True*

F8   How a virus spreads can be completely independent of the payload it executes on each system it infects. *False*

F9   Viruses can spread to systems even with no Internet connectivity. *True*

F10   Worms can spread to systems even with no Internet connectivity. *False*

F11   Viruses can spread even without user interaction/input/action. *False*

F12   Worms cannot spread without some user interaction/input/action. *False*

F13   A Trojan horse cannot send out copies of itself. *False*

F14   A Trojan horse needs a host program to function. *False*

F15   Signature-based detection can detect new malware. *False*

F16   Heuristic detection cannot detect new malware. *False*

F17   While sanitizing files, antivirus software will never destroy the files or adversely affect their functionality. *False*

F18   Trojan malware (usually) uses tracking cookie. *False*

F19   Boot sector virus mostly spreads through removable devices. *True*

F20   Multipartite virus cannot infect the boot sectors. *False*

F21   Multipartite virus can infect the executables. *True*

F22   Multipartite virus can get into a system via multiple media. *True*

F23   Polymorphic virus is not easily detectable by traditional antivirus software. *True*

F24   Polymorphic virus usually changes their signature upon replication. *True*

F25   Trojan malware can self-replicate. *False*

F26   Trojan horses replicate themselves, similar to viruses. *False*

F27   Macro viruses depend on applications for propagation. *True*

F28   A worm can infect a computer even without any user interaction. *True*

F29   A virus can infect a computer even without any user interaction. *False*

F30   A virus usually attaches to header files and propagates. *False*

F31   A worm needs a file to attach to for it to spread. *False*

F32   A computer cannot get infected with a virus by just visiting a Web site. *False*

F33   Real-world malware may have overlapping features/capabilities of different malware categories. *True*

F34   Most antivirus software run within the operating system (OS). **_True_**

F35   A Trojan horse alters the IP address of the computer. **_False_**

F36   A Trojan horse opens backdoor for malicious software. **_True_**

F37   Worms can cause hosts to communicate with each other. **_True_**

F38   Worms cannot perform port scanning. **_False_**

F39   Botnets can be detected by antispyware programs. **_False_**

F40   Rootkits cannot usually be detected by antispyware programs. **_True_**

F41   Rootkit functionality does not require full administrator rights. **_False_**

F42   A multipartite virus is a hybrid of boot and program viruses. **_True_**

F43   Trojans replicate themselves like viruses. **_False_**

F44   Viruses do not infect executable files. **_False_**

F45   A virus cannot infect multiple types of files. **_False_**

F46   There is no type of virus which itself is encrypted. **_False_**

F47   Certain types of viruses can subject themselves to compression/decompression. **_True_**

F48   All functionally equivalent variations of a virus have the same bit patterns / signatures. **_False_**

F49   Viruses infect documents, but not executable files. **_False_**

F50   A worm has the capability of executing a copy of itself on another system. **_True_**

F51   A virus does not have the capability of executing (by itself) a copy of itself on another system. **_True_**

F52   A worm does not have the capability to log onto a remote system as a user. *__False__*

F53   A virus that attaches to an executable program can go beyond the permissions granted to the program. *__False__*

F54   A macro virus infects executable portions of code. *__False__*

F55   Malware code cannot be designed to only infect specific systems. *__False__*

F56   Trojan horse programs can communicate data from the victim's computer to the attacker's computer via email. *__True__*

F57   A computer infected with a Trojan horse program can continue to exhibit normal behavior. *__True__*

F58   A computer infected with a Trojan horse program can deviate from its normal behavior. *__True__*

F59   A Trojan malware only steals (sensitive) user data, but will not modify or destroy data. *__False__*

F60   A malware will never have a nonfunctional payload. *__False__*

F61   Malware is only capable of doing damage to data (corruption) but not damage to physical equipment. *__False__*

F62   Some viruses conceal themselves using encryption. *__True__*

F63   There is no rootkit which can execute in kernel mode. *__False__*

F64   There is no rootkit which can intercept kernel API calls. *__False__*

F65   Malware has never caused physical hardware damage to infected systems. *__False__*

F66   Some viruses are capable of adding their code to that of executables residing on disk. *__True__*

F67   All uses of spyware are illegal. *__False__*

F68   A worm cannot propagate across computers without network(s). **_True_**

F69   A virus can propagate across computers even without the use of network(s). **_True_**

F70   Macro virus can change how the virus is stored on disk. **_True_**

F71   Boot sector virus is self-replicating. **_False_**

F72   There are certain file extensions that are likely to be associated with malware. **_True_**

F73   All malware infected files can be disinfected. **_False_**

F74   Antivirus software cannot stop all malware incidents. **_True_**

F75   Presence of a virus in a computer can damage (or corrupt) data/files even if the infected host file or program is not opened/run. **_False_**

F76   Macros used by word processors and spreadsheets are potential targets for all kinds of viruses. **_False_**

F77   No virus can stay in memory (RAM) all the time. **_False_**

F78   Content filtering may not effectively block highly customized malware. **_True_**

G. Attacks

G1   There is no attack where an attacker can enter a system bypassing the authentication steps. *False*

G2   A flood attack launched with a spoofed address will not consume incoming bandwidth of the attacker. *True*

G3   Spoofing involves redirecting traffic by changing the IP record for a specific domain. *False*

G4   A man-in-the-middle attack usually interrupts the communication between the sender and receiver. *False*

G5   A man-in-the-middle attack intercepts the communication between the sender and receiver. *True*

G6   Availability is compromised in a man-in-the-middle attack. *False*

G7   There is breach of confidentiality in a man-in-the-middle attack. *True*

G8   There is breach of availability in a spoofing attack. *True*

G9   There is no breach of confidentiality in a DoS (Denial of Service) attack. *True*

G10   DoS is an attack on the integrity of data. *False*

G11   Replay attack involves flooding a listening port on a machine with packets in order to disrupt service. *False*

G12   Replay attack is an active attack. *False*

G13   Increasing the amount of time before the resetting an unfinished TCP connection mitigates DDoS attacks. *False*

G14   Setting up filters on external routers to drop all ICMP packets mitigates DDoS attacks. *True*

G15   Setting up a filter that blocks Internet traffic with an internal network address, mitigates DDoS attacks. _**True**_

G16   ARP poisoning involves changing the IP record for a specific domain. _**False**_

G17   ARP poisoning involves broadcasting a fake reply to an entire network. _**True**_

G18   DNS spoofing involves sending a flood of ICMP packets to the host. _**False**_

G19   DoS attack can be carried out at multiple layers of network. _**True**_

G20   SYN flooding is an attack on availability. _**True**_

G21   DNS amplification is an attack the integrity aspect of security. _**False**_

G22   DNS query flooding does not come under the network layer DoS attack. _**True**_

G23   Most commonly, sniffing is an active attack which modifies the data packets passing through a target network. _**False**_

G24   Sniffing interrupts the data/message flowing in/out of a target (victim) computer. _**False**_

G25   Sniffing is capable of capturing router configuration. _**True**_

G26   Sniffing is not capable of capturing web traffic. _**False**_

G27   Sniffing is not an attack on network availability. _**True**_

G28   HTTP, being an application level protocol, is not susceptible to sniffing. _**False**_

G29   SMTP, despite being an application level protocol, is susceptible to sniffing. _**True**_

G30   POP and IMAP being application level protocols, are not susceptible to sniffing. _**False**_

G31   In active sniffing, the network traffic can also be altered to carry out an attack. *True*

G32   Protocol analyzers (devices plugged into a network) monitor traffic, but will not manipulate it. *True*

G33   In a spoofing attack, the attacker does not actively takeover another system to perform the attack. *True*

G34   Session hijacking takes place only at the application level. *False*

G35   Session hijacking can take place at the network level. *True*

G36   Spoofing attacks can be mitigated using IPsec for transmissions between critical servers and clients. *True*

G37   Setting up filters on external routers to drop all incoming ICMP packets mitigates session hijacking. *False*

G38   A telnet session is not prone to man-in-the-middle attack. *False*

G39   Use of different servers for authoritative and recursive lookups helps minimize the effects of DNS poisoning. *True*

G40   In a DoS attack, each packet can potentially be traced back to its source. *True*

G41   In the ping of death (PoD) attack, a flood of well-formed packets is sent to the target machine. *False*

G42   In the ping of death (PoD) attack, a single ping with a packet that is too large for the server to handle can bring down a target system. *True*

G43   Even a properly configured firewall cannot prevent a SYN flood attack. *False*

G44   Man-in-the-middle attack is prevented by using public-key certificates to authenticate the communicating entities. *True*

G45   All the nodes in the botnet can be issued commands and remotely controlled by the originator of the botnet. *True*

G46   Botnets are used for DDoS attacks, but not for spamming. *False*

G47   In a DDoS attack using zombie computers, each of the computers usually acts autonomously. *False*

G48   Attacks are only targeted towards Web servers, but not firewalls. *False*

G49   In an ICMP echo attack where the source address is not spoofed, the attacker gets affected with a flood of packets. *True*

G50   Use of spoofed source addresses does not make it any harder to trace back to the actual attacker. *False*

G51   DHCP snooping is a type of attack using DHCP protocol. *False*

G52   DHCP snooping improves the security of a DHCP infrastructure, while DHCP spoofing is an attack. *True*

G53   All the spoofed (forged) addresses in most of the DoS attacks are valid addresses of real machines. *False*

G54   Amplification attacks do not use spoofed source addresses. *False*

G55   Amplification attacks are the same as reflector attacks. *False*

G56   In the reflector attack, multiple replies (responses) are sent by a Web server (intermediary) for each original packet that is sent to it. *False*

G57   In amplification attack, the original request is sent by the attacker to the broadcast address for some network. *True*

G58   Every flooding attack uses spoofed addresses. *False*

G59   All kinds of network flooding are due to attacks. *False*

G60   Prevention of spoofed source addresses defends against DNS amplification attack. *True*

G61   Prevention of spoofed source addresses does not defend against reflection-based attacks. *False*

G62   In reflection attacks, the source addresses of the packets are spoofed with the IP address of the attacker. *__False__*

G63   In the *ARP spoofing* attack traffic meant for the target host will be sent to the attacker's host. *__True__*

G64   ICMP packets without spoofed source address of the victim are sent by the attacker in *Smurf* attack. *__False__*

G65   SYN flood attack makes it impossible for the victim server to accept new connections. *__True__*

G66   With some type of attack(s) it is possible to shut down a server remotely, without logging onto it. *__False__*

G67   A keylogger can be used as spyware. *__True__*

G68   Denial of Service (DoS) and spoofing attacks are possible in the network layer of the TCP/IP model. *__True__*.

G69   Modification of DNS records results in misdirected traffic. *__True__*

G70   Most *botnets* rely on existing peer-to-peer networks for communication. *__True__*

G71   SQL injection attack requires database administrator privileges. *__False__*

G72   SQL injection attack requires an SQL statement that need not always be true. *__False__*

G73   ARP spoofing is a method of session hijacking. *__True__*

G74   DNS spoofing is a method of session hijacking. *__True__*

G75   A DoS (denial of service) attack will not compromise confidentiality of data. *__True__*

G76   A DoS (denial of service) attack will compromise the integrity of data. *__False__*

G77   The process of changing email message IDs to look as though they came from someone else is known as *spoofing*. *False*

G78   The process of changing IP addresses to look as though they came from some other source is known as *spoofing*. *True*

G79   SYN flooding is an attack on network bandwidth. *True*

G80   SYN flood attack involves malformed packets. *False*

G81   Packets used in an ACK attack do not contain the body (payload) of the packet. *True*

G82   Cross-site scripting injects client-side scripts onto web pages. *True*

G83   Cross-site scripting attack can be prevented by filtering all user input. *True*

G84   The denial of service (DoS) attack attempts to obtain sensitive information from computers. *False*

G85   Leaving a connection half open is a symptom of SYN flood attack. *True*

G86   There are specific kinds of attacks which are targeted toward specific port numbers. *True*

G87   Blocking incoming ICMP packets will prevent Ping scan. *True*

G88   Blocking incoming ICMP packets will prevent SYN flood attack. *False*

G89   Ill-formed requests are attacks on vulnerabilities of Lightweight Directory Access Protocol (LDAP). *True*

G90   SQL injection is a browser-based exploit. *False*

G91   Session hijacking is a browser-based exploit. *True*

G92   Denial of service (DoS) attacks do not happen at transport layer. *False*

G93   Denial of service (DoS) attacks happen only at application layer. ***False***

G94   In SYN flood attack, the connection requests will have attacker's source address. ***False***

G95   Spoofing a TCP packet is no more difficult than spoofing a UDP packet. ***False***

G96   The effort required in spoofing a UDP packet and spoofing a TCP packet are about the same. ***False***

G97   Spoofing a TCP packet is significantly more difficult than spoofing a UDP packet. ***True***

G98   Spoofing a TCP packet requires correct sequence numbers in addition to correct port numbers. ***True***

G99   Eavesdropping is not possible in a secure Ethernet network. ***True***

G100   Attacker can inject forged packets in a secure Ethernet network. ***True***

G101   A packet sniffer can monitor network activity and determine possibility of a DoS attack. ***True***

G102   The serial port of a computer is not a potential entry point for malicious code. ***False***

G103   Use of static mapping for IP addresses and ARP tables are effective methods to mitigate ARP poisoning. ***False***

G104   Networking devices and services installed with a default set of user credentials are easy targets for attacks. ***True***

G105   Backdoors are usually inserted after the system is deployed. ***False***

G106   SSID (service set identifier) broadcast can most likely cause privilege escalation. ***False***

G107   Application flaws are most likely causes of privilege escalation. ***True***

G108 A rootkit cannot provide escalated privileges (administrative rights). *False*

G109 An attacker can do a successful port scan to determine the open TCP ports on a target host by sending packets that have a spoofed IP address. *False*

G110 An attacker doing a port scan with spoofed address in order to hide its identity will never know of open ports. *True*

G111 In IP spoofing, the source and destination addresses in the sender's IP datagram are interchanged by the attacker. *False*

G112 Messages can only be sent from the attacker to a bot (malware), and not the other way. *False*

G113 The purpose of the nonce is to defend against the replay attack. *True*

G114 After a fix for a known vulnerability has been developed, it is no longer considered a *zero-day vulnerability*. *True*

G115 The primary defense against many DoS attacks is to prevent source address spoofing. *True*

G116 In the ciphertext-only attack the attacker has the least amount of information to work with. *True*

G117 The propagation and activation of bots is usually controlled from a central remote system. *True*

G118 A bot has its own distinct IP address. *True*

G119 The denial of service (DoS) attack only exhausts the communication bandwidth, but not CPU, memory, and disk space. *False*

G120 Anomaly detection techniques are well suited for tackling denial-of-service (DoS) attacks. *True*

G121 Presence of worms and spreading of worms can be detected by anomaly detection techniques. *True*

G122   The way a virus spreads is dependent on the payload it executes on each system it infects. *False*

G123   Cryptanalytic attacks use mostly brute force than mathematical techniques. *False*

G124   Malware transmission attack is carried out at the network layer. *False*

G125   Scans for vulnerable ports are carried out at the network layer. *False*

G126   Scanning (passive attack) is done only at the transport layer. *False*

G127   Use of public-key/certificate authority will thwart a man-in-the-middle attack. *True*

G128   An attacker cannot eavesdrop on the TCP connection and observe the sequence numbers on any network. *False*

G129   In source routing, traffic can be directed through machine(s) controlled by attacker. *True*

G130   The AH protocol of IPSec cannot provide protection against replay attacks. *False*

G131   Cross-site (XSS) attacks can never be used to exploit vulnerabilities in the victim's web browser. *False*

H. Network Security

H1   In link encryption, the packet body (payload part of message) is also encrypted. *False*

H2   It is not possible for a packet to pass through TCP layer but get rejected by the SSL. *False*

H3   Onion routing prevents any intermediate node from knowing the true source and destination of communication. *True*

H4   With link encryption, the header of a packet stays encrypted even inside a switch/router. *False*

H5   With link encryption, the header of a packet is encrypted/decrypted at the intermediary nodes. *True*

H6   With end–to–end encryption, the packet header is encrypted/decrypted at the intermediary nodes along the route. *False*

H7   With end–to–end encryption, the packet payload (body) is encrypted/decrypted at the sender/receiver hosts. *True*

H8   With link encryption, the packet body (payload/part of message) isencrypted before sending out on each link. *False*

H9   With end–to–end encryption, the packet header is encrypted at the sending node. *False*

H10   With end–to–end encryption, the packet body is encrypted/decrypted at the intermediate nodes. *False*

H11   The connectionless protocol usually uses more new session keys in a given time than the connection–oriented protocol. *True*

H12   Port scanning is used to determine ports on a target which are running and responding. *True*

H13   In VPN, the same header information of a packet in a private network can be used for routing in the public network. *False*

H14   IPSec implementation requires changes to TCP, UDP, and Applications layers. *False*

H15   TCP checks only for transmission errors and not for security related errors. *True*

H16   For connection-oriented protocol, a new session key is used for each data exchange during the connection. *False*

H17   In end-to-end encryption, the packet body is encrypted/decrypted only at the source/destination nodes. *True*

H18   In end-to-end encryption, the packet header is encrypted. *False*

H19   A *network-based* IDS also monitors activities within host computers. *False*

H20   A *host-based* IDS does not monitor network traffic. *True*

H21   A packet that has the same source and destination IP address is suspicious. *True*

H22   The address resolution protocol (ARP) does not have any protection against ARP attacks. *True*

H23   It is not possible to insert code by hackers into ICMP protocol which is just used to send status information. *False*

H24   A network router creates a new header for each packet that it moves forward. *True*

H25   The routing tables at the routers are based on MAC addresses. *False*

H26   A router does not forward broadcast packets. *True*

H27   A bridge does not forward broadcast packets. *False*

H28   A router uses the same network address for all ports. *False*

H29   Authentication header (AH) protocol provides protection from replay attacks. *True*

H30   End-to-end connection takes place in the data link layer. *False*

H31   IP protocol is a connection-oriented protocol. *False*

H32   Thwarting SYN flood attack can be done by the use of SYN proxies. *True*

H33   Packet filtering firewall cannot be configured to discard all packets using source routing option. *False*

H34   Packets arriving from outside the network with source addresses of hosts within the network are very likely packets with spoofed (forged) source addresses. *True*

H35   Packets arriving from outside the network with source addresses of hosts within the network are (likely) not part of an attack. *False*

H36   TLS (Transport Level Security) makes use of certificates. *True*

H37   TLS uses asymmetric cryptography to encrypt the messages. *False*

H38   Both communicating parties of using TLS participate in key generation. *True*

H39   A TLS session uses more than one key for data transfer data from a client to a server. *True*

H40   TCP traffic can easily be filtered with a stateful packet filter by enforcing the context or state of the request. *True*

H41   ICMP traffic can easily be filtered with a stateful packet filter by enforcing the context or state of the request. *False*

H42   UDP traffic cannot be filtered with a stateful packet filter by enforcing the context or state of the request. *True*

H43   SSL is not vulnerable to denial-of-service attack. *False*

H44   SSL (or TLS) cannot by itself trigger a re-transmission of packets. *True*

H45   It is never the case that (at a destination) a packet is accepted by the TCP layer but is rejected by the SSL layer. *False*

H46   A corrupted SSL payload may still have a packet with a correct sequence number and TCP checksum. *True*

H47   TCP connection initiation requests from an external host to a local host could be blocked by a firewall, while the returning traffic from an external host to a local host for its initiation requests is allowed. *True*

H48   It is never the case that SYN-packets from an external host to a local host are filtered out, while SYN-ACK packets from an external host to a local host are allowed. *False*

H49   In VPN, the body and header of a packet in a private network is encapsulated as a payload in another packet and new header is added before sending onto a public network. *True*

H50   Tunnel mode IPSec is commonly used in remote-access VPN. *False*

H51   Transport mode IPSec is commonly used in remote-access VPN. *True*

H52   In the transport mode of VPN, individual hosts do not encrypt the packets. *False*

H53   In the tunnel mode of VPN, individual hosts encrypt the packets. *False*

H54   Multiple systems can never share a single IP address. *False*

H55   Support for IPSec is optional in IPv4. *True*

H56   Support for IPSec is mandatory in IPv6. *True*

H57   Secure socket layer (SSL) is a connectionless protocol. *False*

H58   In transport mode of VPN, IPSec encrypts only the packet payload. *True*

H59   In transport mode of VPN, the headers are unencrypted. **_True_**

H60   In tunnel mode of VPN, IPSec encrypts only the packet payload. **_False_**

H61   The encapsulating security payload (ESP) part of IPSec provides confidentiality. **_True_**

H62   The encapsulating security protection (ESP) of IPSec does not provide authentication. **_False_**

H63   The Authentication Header (AH) of IPSec provides confidentiality. **_False_**

H64   The ESP protocol of IPSec does not encrypt the IP addresses. **_True_**

H65   Authentication header (AH) protocol of IPSec provides data integrity and data origin authentication. **_True_**

H66   Encapsulating security payloads (ESP) protocol of IPSec provides confidentiality, data origin authentication, and data integrity. **_True_**

H67   IPSec also has a protocol for the compression of packet payload. **_True_**

H68   TLS uses a different keys for encrypting traffic in the client-to-server direction and in the server-to-client direction. **_False_**

H69   A TLS client confirms the validity of a certificate received from a server by verifying that the server signed the certificate. **_False_**

H70   TLS provides protection against TCP RST injection attacks. **_False_**

H71   UDP does not use any encryption. **_True_**

H72   DNS uses symmetric encryption. **_False_**

H73   TLS uses both symmetric and asymmetric encryption. **_True_**

H74   Port scanning does not use any encryption. **_True_**

H75   ARP uses symmetric encryption. **_False_**

H76 HTTP uses symmetric encryption. ***False***

H77 ESP encrypts only the data payload of each packet. ***True***

H78 ESP provides for integrity, authentication and encryption to IP datagrams. ***True***

H79 AH provides integrity and authentication for IP datagrams. ***True***

H80 One security association is adequate for bi-directional communication between two IPSec systems. ***False***

H81 VPN does not use the Internet protocol security (IPSec). ***False***

H82 Internet protocol security (IPSec) encrypts only the packet data, but not the header information. ***False***

H83 Internet protocol security (IPSec) provides protection against unauthorized retransmission of packets. ***True***

H84 Telnet is an end-to-end protocol. ***True***

H85 Internet Protocol (IP) is an end-to-end protocol. ***False***

H86 In an end-to-end protocol, the intermediate hosts are involved in forwarding the messages only. ***True***

H87 In an end-to-end protocol, encryption/decryption of messages is done at all the hosts along the path from the source to the destination. ***False***

H88 In a link protocol, encryption/decryption is done at each host along the path from the source to the destination. ***True***

H89 The SSL record protocol provides both confidentiality and message integrity. ***True***

H90 In SSL record protocol, the MAC (message authentication code) is computed on the message blocks before compression. ***False***

H91 SSL handles packet retransmission and reliable packet delivery. ***False***

H92   SSL does not authenticate the message to the recipient. *__True__*

H93   An SSL record is always contained within a single TCP segment. *__True__*

H94   Multiple SSL records may be sent in a single TCP segment. *__True__*

H95   The sequence number in the header of a message is changed in transit from source to destination via several intermediate hosts. *__False__*

H96   The time to live (TTL) field in the header of a message can change in transit from source to destination via several intermediate hosts. *__True__*

H97   Port scanning can be done via a TCP connection request. *__True__*

H98   Port scanning cannot be done via a UDP datagram. *__False__*

H99   Encryption is a primary defense against sniffing. *__True__*

H100   SSL provides protection against SYN flood attack. *__False__*

H101   The secure socket layer (SSL) protocol is asymmetric (the communicating parties have different roles). *__True__*

H102   The secure socket layer (SSL) protocol provides confidentiality, but not authentication. *__False__*

H103   The secure socket layer (SSL) protocol always provides server authentication. *__True__*

H104   The secure socket layer (SSL) protocol always provides client authentication. *__False__*

H105   TLS typically only provides one-way authentication (the server authenticating to client). *__True__*

H106   In TLS, messages are encrypted using public-key encryption. *__False__*

H107 In TLS, the clients (usually) authenticate themselves to the server. *False*

H108 IPSec encrypts only the TCP segment but not the UDP segment. *False*

H109 Using IPsec a new SA will be established for each packet sent in the stream. *False*

H110 In IPSec, all the packets sent between the hosts will use the established SAs with the same session keys. *True*

H111 Retransmission of the same segment by TCP running over IPSec will have the same sequence number in the IPsec headers. *False*

H112 IPsec at the source increments the sequence number for every new datagram sent by the source. *True*

H113 It is never the case that the same segment will be sent within different diagrams with different sequence numbers. *False*

H114 An open port always responds to a TCP SYN message. *True*

H115 Secure socket layer (SSL) makes use of digital certificates. *True*

H116 IPSec does not use digital certificates. *False*

H117 Transport layer security (TLS) and secure socket layer (SSL) provide complete protection against traffic analysis. *False*

H118 IPSec is below the transport layer and transparent to applications. *True*

H119 IPSec is optional in IPv6. *False*

H120 In Tor (The onion router), the IP addresses of the nodes are encrypted. *True*

H121 In Tor, some nodes may not have an identifying IP address. *False*

H122 In Tor, the only IP address visible to the destination is that of the final node (exit node).

H123   With the use of Tor, the packets arriving at the destination node cannot be traced back to the original source node. _**True**_

H124   Even while using Tor, the Internet Service Provider (ISP) can determine the traffic contents and websites visited. _**False**_

H125   An intercepted packet in transit in onion routing can never reveal the origin or destination. _**True**_

H126   In TCP, data is sent unencrypted. _**True**_

H127   There cannot be multiple IP addresses as response for a queried host name from a DNS authoritative server. _**False**_

H128   TCP connection initiation requests from an internal host to an external host may not always be allowed by a firewall. _**True**_

H129   TCP sequence numbers can prevent spoofing. _**False**_

H130   While establishing a TCP connection, the client and the server share the initial sequence number (ISN). _**False**_

H131   In some systems, the IP address of a device can change while it is still connected. _**True**_

H132   Hosts using Dynamic Host Configuration Protocol (DHCP) on a wired network (ex. Ethernet) are immune to possible DHCP spoofing attacks. _**False**_

H133   TLS is not (generally) used to secure DNS. _**True**_

H134   DNSSEC does not hide the names that are looked up nor for their replies. _**True**_

H135   HTTPS does not mask the IP addresses of the clients nor of the servers. _**True**_

H136   SSL operates at the application layer. _**False**_

H137   SSL uses implicit sequence numbers. _**True**_

H138 IPsec will increment the sequence number for every packet it sends. **_True_**

H139 An SSL handshake takes place before a TCP connection is established. **_False_**

H140 Session keys are established between two communicating entities during SSL handshake. **_True_**

H141 Authentication of two communicating entities (ex. server and client) is done during SSL handshake. **_True_**

H142 SSL primarily focuses on maintaining the integrity of the data. **_False_**

H143 VPNs can hide browsing activities of users and maintain anonymity. **_True_**

H144 VPNs can mask IP addresses of users and maintain anonymity. **_True_**

H145 There is always a one-to-one mapping of hostnames to IP addresses. **_False_**

H146 Many hostnames may correspond to a single IP address. **_True_**

H147 A single hostname may not correspond to many IP addresses. **_False_**

H148 Changes to the local DNS settings by malware could redirect the user to malicious sites. **_True_**

H149 When host *A* sends a SYN packet to request TCP connection to host *B* with a spoofed source address, host *A* can still receive the SYN+ACK packet from *B*. **_False_**

H150 Using Network Address Translation (NAT), IP addresses of internal hosts of a network are not visible to outside hosts. **_True_**

H151 SSL and TLS provide essentially the same end-to-end security. **_True_**

H152   ICMP scanning is used for checking live systems. *True*

H153   Not every running/live host responds to ICMP ECHO requests. *False*

H154   VPNs facilitate preservation of privacy of its users. *True*

H155   Network mapper is a tool that can be used for creating an inventory of services hosted on networked systems. *False*

H156   Port scanner is a tool that can be used for creating an inventory of services hosted on networked systems. *True*

H157   Protocol analyzer is an assessment tool for checking particular versions and patch levels of a service. *False*

H158   Protocol analyzer is an assessment tool that reports information used to identify single points of failure. *False*

H159   Vulnerability scanner is an assessment tool that reports information used to identify single points of failure. *False*

H160   Network mapper is an assessment tool that reports information used to identify single points of failure. *True*

H161   Port scanner is also often referred to as packet sniffer. *False*

H162   Vulnerability scanner is also often referred to as packet sniffer. *False*

H163   S-HTTP and HTTPS communicate over the same ports. *False*

H164   Small key size is a vulnerability associated with SSL certificates. *True*

H165   Outdated certificate revocation lists (CRLs) are vulnerabilities associated with SSL certificates. *True*

H166   Network mapper is a software utility that scans a single machine or a range of IP addresses. *False*

H167   Tool such as *WireShark* can detect the presence of malware in a computer. ***False***

H168   Reverse DNS lookup can be used to identify SPAM emails. ***True***

H169   SSL uses public key cryptography. ***True***

H170   Blocking all incoming ICMP packets cannot be done. ***False***

H171   The sender includes an index into the security association table in every packet. ***True***

H172   Link layer encryption is not appropriate for communicating parties without a direct connection. ***True***

H173   Adding security to the packets at the network layer requires modifications to the applications / application layer. ***False***

H174   Under IPSec, the packets are guaranteed to arrive at the destination in the order they were sent from the source. ***False***

H175   The ESP and AH protocols of IPSec must be used together on IP packets. ***False***

H176   The AH authentication of IPSec authenticates the entire IP packet (including the outer IP header). ***True***

H177   When using the AH protocol, the type of payload (TCP, UDP, ICMP, etc.) is specified in the AH header. ***False***

H178   With the ESP protocol, an intruder cannot determine the type of payload (TCP, UDP, ICMP, etc.) because the payload type is encrypted. ***True***

H179   Multiple systems can never share a single IP address. ***False***

H180   In HTTPS, URL of the requested document is encrypted. ***True***

H181   In HTTPS, cookies sent between server and browser are not encrypted. ***False***

H182   In HTTPS, the contents of the document transferred are encrypted. *True*

H183   In HTTPS, the contents of the forms (filled in by user) are not encrypted. *False*

H184   HTTP over SSL and HTTP over TLS are significantly different. *False*

H185   IPSec works at the transport layer (TCP, UDP). *False*

H186   IPSec can detect and reject replayed packets. *True*

H187   SSL provides no protection against SYN flooding attack. *True*

H188   A packet that successfully passes through the TCP layer at the receiver could be rejected by the SSL. *True*

H189   A packet passes through the TCP layer if it has the correct checksum. *True*

H190   Penetration test will never cause any disruption to network operations. *False*

H191   Port scanners compile a list of all hardware present within a network segment. *False*

H192   Port scanners test only for the availability of services. *True*

H193   Vulnerability scanners check for a particular version or patch level of a service. *True*

H194   Vulnerability scanners compile a list of all hardware present within a network segment. *False*

H195   No connection can be established without specifying a username or password. *False*

H196   ARP (address resolution protocol) does not require any type of validation. *True*

H197   An ARP reply is added to ARP cache without any type of verification. *True*

H198   Bastian hosts provide most of the standard services that are normally provided on a host. *False*

H199   Host computers of a protected network are placed in the demilitarized zone (DMZ). *False*

H200   The very essential servers (ex. Web server, email server) are placed in the demilitarized zone (DMZ). *True*

H201   The return addresses in the headers of all packets leaving a network (intranet) using a proxy server are not modified. *False*

H202   Onion-routing schemes (ex. Tor) use a distinct cryptographic key for each hop from the source to destination through the network. *True*

H203   Passive eavesdropping is easier on UDP traffic than on TCP traffic. *False*

H204   An Internet Service Provider (ISP) cannot link IP address with personal information (name, address, etc.). *False*

H205   Individual users can connect to private networks at home and access resources remotely using *router-to-router* VPNs. *False*

H206   In the ARP protocol a host can authenticate the peer from which the packet originated. *False*

H207   In the HTTP connection data is never encrypted and sent as plain-text. *True*

H208   *Telnet* which is used for remote login uses encrypted text messages. *False*

H209   Secure Hypertext Transport Protocol (S-HTTP) operates over port 80 along with regular HTTP traffic. *True*

H210   Data transfer using HTTP (hypertext transfer protocol) is unencrypted. *True*

H211   In The Onion Router (Tor), the data traffic is subjected to layers of encryption, each layer controlled by a different node. **_True_**

H212   The DMZ systems never face attacks from the internal protected network since they belong to the same organization. **_False_**

H213   Security controls exist at each layer of the TCP/IP model. **_True_**

H214   ISPs need to ensure that the packets going out to the Internet have addresses in the valid range. **_True_**

H215   Application layer security mechanisms can protect application data as well as lower level information such as IP addresses. **_False_**

H216   S-HTTP (Secure Hypertext Transport Protocol) and HTTPS (HTTP over SSL) are the same. **_False_**

H217   Secure Hypertext Transport Protocol (S-HTTP) operates over port other than regular HTTP traffic (port 80). **_False_**

H218   Scanning can be done at multiple (application, transport, network) layers of the network. **_True_**

H219   ISPs (Internet Service Providers) cannot cache HTTPS traffic. **_True_**

H220   Examining the source IP address is sufficient to determine where the message came from. **_False_**

H221   Configuration of routers will not have no effect on vulnerabilities. **_False_**

H222   In connection–oriented protocols, usually the same session key is used for the duration the connection is open. **_True_**

I. Web Security and Application Security

I1   When a link to a Web server is clicked on in a browser, data from several other sites may also be loaded. ***True***

I2   Support for add-ins and plug-ins in browsers could cause vulnerabilities. ***True***

I3   The SET (Secure Electronic Transaction) is a payment system. ***False***

I4   SQL statements can be used by attackers to bypass authentication. ***True***

I5   A cookie is an executable script or program. ***False***

I6   PGP (Pretty Good Privacy) is a security mechanism for email. ***True***

I7   PGP (Pretty Good Privacy) does not provide authentication. ***False***

I8   After Radix–64 conversion (in PGP), there will be data expansion. ***True***

I9   PGP message is encrypted with a one–time session key. ***True***

I10   PGP (Pretty Good Privacy) does not provide authentication. ***False***

I11   PGP message is encrypted with the receiver's public key. ***False***

I12   The public–key ring (in PGP) of a user consists of the public keys of the user. ***False***

I13   The key ID in the private–key ring (in PGP) is the least significant 64 bits of the private key. ***False***

I14   *All* cookies are stored permanently on the hard disk. ***False***

I15   Some cookies are erased from the Web browser's memory at the end of a session. ***True***

I16   Rule-based access control is not necessarily identity-based. ***True***

I17   It is not possible to configure a database so users can or cannot see at the granularity of fields within database records. ***False***

I18   Decisions about access of objects are made solely on the identity of the subject. ***False***

I19   Decisions about access of objects are made solely on the sensitivity of object's content. ***False***

I20   Cookies pose the risks of personal data collection and impersonation. ***True***

I21   A cookie can keep track of every website that a user visits. ***False***

I22   Typically the only site which can access a cookie file is the site that created it. ***True***

I23   A cookie file only contains information about the user related to the particular site that created the cookie. ***True***

I24   A cookie in a computer can track all activities on it. ***False***

I25   A cookie in a computer can adversely affect the computer's performance. ***False***

I26   A cookie can sometimes destroy information in the computer. ***False***

I27   A user has the option to not permit cookies to be stored on the computer. ***True***

I28   Cookies could pose data integrity threats. ***False***

I29   Cookies could pose data confidentiality threats. ***False***

I30   Cookies pose risks of breach of privacy. ***True***

I31   Cookies are not required (mandatory) for all Web pages to work properly. ***False***

I32 Using a stolen cookie the account can be accessed from some Web sites without needing login details (provided the cookie has not expired or changed since it was stolen). *True*

I33 The Simple Mail Transfer Protocol (SMTP) does not provide authentication. *True*

I34 The Simple Mail Transfer Protocol (SMTP) provides message integrity check. *False*

I35 The Simple Mail Transfer Protocol (SMTP) does not support non-repudiation. *True*

I36 PGP does not provide sender authentication. *False*

I37 PGP provides non-repudiation. *True*

I38 Cookies may store authentication data. *True*

I39 PGP provides confidentiality (via encryption), but not authentication. *False*

I40 All browsers keep the passwords saved in them in encrypted format. *False*

I41 The bytes transmitted by two web clients to the server when retrieving the same URL from a given HTTPS server will be identical. *False*

I42 TLS uses the same key (for a client-server pair) for encrypting traffic in both the client-to-server and server-to-client directions. *False*

I43 TLS provides protection against TCP reset attacks. *False*

I44 Fetching a given URL over HTTPS takes the same amount of time as in HTTP. *False*

I45 In SET (Secure Electronic Transaction), the merchant has access to payment information. *False*

I46   Browser requests to the server never contain personal information. *False*

I47   Web server response to browser never contains malicious (unsafe) code. *False*

I48   A cookie is never sent from the browser (client) to the Web server. *False*

I49   Typically, no Web site other than the one that created the cookie can read it. *True*

I50   All cookies reside on the client (browser) until explicitly deleted by the user. *False*

I51   Cookies can only be placed by Web servers that a user is visiting directly. *False*

I52   Web servers in domains other than the one a user is visiting directly, can also place cookies in the client (browser). *True*

I53   Browser (client) always send the cookie to Web server over HTTPS. *False*

I54   In SQL injection attack, the malicious data goes from the server to the browser (client). *False*

I55   Web application penetration testing can check for URL manipulation vulnerability. *True*

I56   Web application penetration testing cannot check for SQL injection vulnerability. *False*

I57   Web application penetration testing cannot check for session hijacking vulnerability. *False*

I58   Web application penetration testing can check for vulnerabilities in web server configuration. *True*

I59   Web application penetration testing can check for cross site scripting vulnerabilities. *True*

I60   Web application penetration testing cannot check for buffer overflow vulnerabilities. *False*

I61   It is not possible to configure client browsers to block all cookies. *False*

I62   Disabling third-party browser extensions is an effective method to mitigate buffer overflows. *False*

I63   Disabling third-party browser extensions is not an effective method to mitigate cross-site scripting attacks. *True*

I64   Blocking third-party cookies is not an effective method to mitigate buffer overflows. *True*

I65   Blocking third-party cookies is an effective method to mitigate cross-site scripting attacks. *False*

I66   Tracking cookie is used by spyware. *True*

I67   Cookies are executable files. *False*

I68   Cookies are used for the purpose of spying on the browsing patterns of users. *False*

I69   The primary purpose of cookies is to provide convenience to users by way of not having to retype several pieces of information while using a Web service. *True*

I70   The data in the cookies can be used to reveal browsing patterns of users. *True*

I71   Misuse of cookies may lead to compromise of privacy. *True*

I72   Cookies cannot be misused for impersonation. *False*

I73   The cookie is an executable file. *False*

I74   The cookie is stored on the Web server. *False*

I75   The cookie is stored on the client computer. *True*

I76   A cookie can be associated with more than one Web site. *False*

I77   The information in a cookie is never transmitted from the browser to the Web server. *False*

I78   The information in a persistent cookie is transmitted to the Web server every time the user visits the website belonging to the server. *True*

I79   A cookie, which is a plaintext file, cannot be misused as spyware. *False*

I80   Just visiting certain (malicious) Web sites will download spyware on the client computer. *True*

I81   Cookies can be used for authentication of browser clients. *True*

I82   A stolen cookie cannot be used to impersonate the user/entity (from whom it was stolen). *False*

I83   Pretty good privacy (PGP) does not use digital certificates. *False*

I84   PGP uses a certificate authority to issue digital certificates. *False*

I85   In PGP, individual users issue and manage their digital certificates. *True*

I86   Certificates used in PGP can have multiple signatures. *True*

I87   Every Web site on the Internet is visible to a search engine. *False*

I88   Use of private window, or incognito mode prevents browsing history from being stored. *True*

I89   In a null session the connection is authenticated. *False*

I90   Cookies can be used to mitigate cross-site scripting (XSS). *True*

I91   Clicking on something malicious on a pop-up window will not infect the computer. *False*

I92   SSL provides encryption of server messages only. *False*

I93   Provision of client authentication in SSL is optional. **_True_**

I94   For public-key certification, PGP uses certification authorities. **_False_**

I95   PGP uses public-key encryption for message encryption. **_False_**

I96   Pretty good privacy (PGP) is not well suited for secure communication between a Web server and client. **_True_**

I97   PGP uses public key cryptography to encrypt the messages. **_False_**

I98   In PGP, compression of the message is done after encryption. **_False_**

I99   In PGP, compression of the message before encryption results in faster encryption. **_True_**

I100   Email filters operate on inbound email traffic only. **_False_**

I101   Software updates are usually sent unencrypted. **_True_**

I102   Software updates sent unencrypted are usually accompanied by message authentic code (MAC) to ensure integrity. **_True_**

I103   Backdoors can be inserted during system testing and integration. **_False_**

I104   Unremoved shortcut entry points inserted during code development to allow rapid evaluation and testing cannot be used to gain unauthorized access. **_False_**

I105   A tracking cookie typically stays much longer than a session cookie. **_True_**

I106   FTP servers support anonymous file access and unencrypted authentication. **_True_**

I107   CGI (common gateway interface) scripts run on the client system. **_False_**

I108   CGI scripts may be exploited to leak details about running server processes and daemons. *True*

I109   While using an anonymizing proxy server, the Internet Service Provider (ISP) will still be able to see the URLs the web pages browsed by the user. *False*

I110   While using an anonymizing proxy server, the Internet Service Provider (ISP) will not be able to see the contents of the web pages browsed by the user. *True*

I111   Most of the transactions in e-commerce use only one-way authentication. *True*

I112   In the e-commerce transactions using only one-way authentication, the business Website (server) has to authenticate the user (client/browser). *False*

I113   Validation of input to remove hypertext prevents cross-site scripting. *True*

I114   In S/MIME, the message body is not encrypted for every message. *True*

I115   In S/MIME, the public key scheme is used for message encryption. *False*

I116   The one-time session key used to encrypt the message in S/MIME is just a large random number. *True*

I117   RSA public-key encryption algorithm cannot be for the digital signature of S/MIME messages. *False*

I118   A malicious Website will infect all clients (browsers) visiting that site. *False*

I119   Some Websites continue to provide their intended functionalities despite the presence malware in them. *True*

I120   Despite the computer of the 'victim' being secure (not vulnerable), a drive-by download attack can succeed. *False*

I121   A user has to download some files from a compromised web site in order for a drive-by download attack to happen. *False*

I122   After a browser accepts cookie from a Web server, all future requests to that server will be accompanied by that cookie. *True*

I123   Cookies can reveal personal information (name, address, etc.). *False*

I124   Whitelisting by way of allowing only well-defined set of safe values can prevent SQL injection attack. *True*

I125   Clustering reduces the likelihood of a single point of failure when a server fails. *True*

I126   S/MIME (Secure/multipurpose internet mail extension) certificates are the basis of single sign-on applications. *True*

I127   Post office protocol (POP) periodically checks the mail-box for synchronizing the latest emails with that of the server. *True*

I128   Both HTTP and HTTPS content cannot be downloaded to browser while displaying in the same page. *False*

I129   Unencrypted email when sent over an IPSec or TLS connection is protected during transmission. *True*

I130   Unencrypted email when sent over an IPSec or TLS connection is unprotected in the intermediate servers along the way. *True*

J. Firewalls and Intrusion Detection

J1   Default configurations of firewalls are more vulnerable to attacks. **_True_**

J2   Firewalls cannot help prevent worms from propagating. **_False_**

J3   Proxy server gateways can act as firewalls. **_False_**

J4   A proxy server can be made to work as a firewall. **_True_**

J5   Firewalls do not control the outgoing traffic. **_False_**

J6   A firewall may be implemented in routers connecting intranets to Internet. **_True_**

J7   A personal computer (PC) cannot be used as a firewall. **_False_**

J8   The same machine cannot be used both as a firewall and proxy server. **_False_**

J9   The headers of all packets leaving a network (intranet) with a proxy server are unchanged **_False_**.

J10   A honeypot is always placed outside the external firewall. **_False_**

J11   Firewalls cannot prevent all DoS attacks. **_True_**

J12   Firewalls can prevent some DoS attacks by blocking all incoming ICMP packets. **_True_**

J13   Any firewall can block every attack. **_False_**

J14   A packet filtering firewall does not make use of information from previous packets. **_True_**

J15   A Stateful Packet Inspection (SPI) firewall can examine the actual contents of a packet. **_True_**

J16   Packet filtering firewalls work well for small networks. **_True_**

J17   Packet filtering firewalls are robust against spoofing attacks. *False*

J18   Packet filtering firewalls cannot support the complex models of rules. *True*

J19   Circuit-level gateway firewalls monitor TCP sessions. *True*

J20   Circuit-level gateway firewalls do not filter packets individually. *True*

J21   It is possible for an attacker to get past the circuit-level gateway firewall. *True*

J22   A spam filter with *false positives* never blocks valid messages from being delivered. *False*

J23   A spam filter with *false negatives* could allow invalid (undesirable) messages to be delivered. *True*

J24   Bayesian filtering typically considers just the message content but not the message header. *False*

J25   Packet filter firewalls cannot look at application-level data. *False*

J26   Filtering outbound traffic helps control DDoS attacks. *True*

J27   Some protocols use dynamically assigned port numbers. *True*

J28   Protocols using dynamically assigned port numbers can be supported with a stateless packet filter. *False*

J29   Packet filtering firewalls examine only the packet header information. *True*

J30   Proxy servers facilitate more extensive traffic logging than packet-filtering firewalls. *True*

J31   Proxies facilitate more intelligent filtering and control over traffic. *True*

J32 Application-level gateways have lower maintenance overhead and performance penalty compared to packet-filtering firewalls. ***False***

J33 SPI (stateful packet inspection) firewalls can detect several SYN packets coming from the same IP address and prevent SYN flood attacks. ***True***

J34 The filtering rules are applied *before* parsing the datagram headers by packet filters. ***False***

J35 Packet filters can defend against network mapping. ***True***

J36 Packet filters cannot defend against DDoS attacks. ***False***

J37 The default *deny* policy of a firewall is comparatively less restrictive. ***False***

J38 Whitelisting of spam filters has similar advantages as 'default deny' of firewalls. ***True***

J39 Spam filters configured to use blacklist is more restrictive than use of whitelist. ***False***

J40 With the use of whitelisting of spam filters, there are no 'false positives' (a genuine sender never gets blocked). ***False***

J41 With the use of 'default deny' in firewalls, there are no 'false negatives' (message from a malicious site is never allowed). ***True***

J42 A firewall at the network perimeter will not provide protection against malicious insiders. ***True***

J43 Firewall on end host machine will not provide protection against outside attackers. ***False***

J44 A firewall will always allow returning traffic initiated by internal hosts. ***False***

J45 It is potentially more difficult to manage policies on firewalls at the network perimeter than on firewalls at end host machines. ***False***

J46   Stateful inspection is also called dynamic packet filtering. **_True_**

J47   Improper configuration of a firewall could impact system vulnerability. **_True_**

J48   Blacklisting is more restrictive than whitelisting in allowing connections. **_False_**

J49   A stateless firewall keeps information about existing connections and TCP sequence numbers. **_False_**

J50   Default firewalls are provided by some vendors with their operating systems. **_True_**

J51   Firewalls need not examine each of the data packets that are leaving the internal network for secure operation. **_False_**

J52   Packet filtering firewalls could be deployed on routers. **_True_**

J53   Some firewalls can filter packets based on the name of a particular protocol (as opposed to the usual port numbers). **_True_**

J54   Packet filtering needs to be done at the destination and not at the source. **_False_**

J55   Every packet is not checked against the network administrator-defined rule set in the packet filtering firewall. **_False_**

J56   Packet filtering technique could support the complex models of rules. **_False_**

J57   Packet filtering technique is sometimes prone to spoofing attacks. **_True_**

J58   Firewalls cannot be at the application layer. **_False_**

J59   Firewalls cannot provide access control services. **_False_**

J60   Firewalls can operate only at the network layer in the TCP/IP protocol stack. **_False_**

J61   Packet filtering firewall applies a set of rules to each incoming packets only, but not to outgoing packets. _**False**_

J62   The packet filter rules are typically defined on the fields of packet headers. _**True**_

J63   The packet filter rules are typically not defined on packet payloads. _**True**_

J64   Packet filter firewalls cannot prevent attacks targeting application-specific vulnerabilities. _**True**_

J65   With the use of application level gateway, there is no end-to-end TCP connection between the hosts. _**True**_

J66   With the use of circuit level gateway, there is end-to-end TCP connection between the hosts. _**False**_

J67   Application-level gateways tend to be more secure than packet filters. _**True**_

J68   Firewall functionality can be implemented as a software module in a router. _**True**_

J69   The external firewall adds more stringent filtering capability compared to the internal firewall. _**False**_

J70   Services available on the inside of a firewall are never subject to attacks. _**False**_

J71   A firewall could consist of two or more systems cooperating and performing the firewall function. _**True**_

J72   A packet filtering firewall typically only filters packets coming from the Internet to a computer (or a private network), but not the outgoing packets. _**False**_

J73   Application-level gateway has additional processing overhead on each connection. _**True**_

J74   Filtering of packets with spoofed source addresses can be more effective when it is done as close to the packet source as possible. *True*

J75   Computers in the local intranet behind the firewall are not 'visible' to other computers on the Internet. *True*

J76   Internet usage logs (audits) is not part of any firewall. *False*

J77   Signature-based Intrusion Detection System (IDS) uses 'if–then' rules. *False*

J78   Intrusion Detection System (IDS) is not effective in mitigating ARP poisoning. *False*

J79   IDS allows identification of malicious activity after it has occurred. *True*

J80   Rule-based intrusion detection is effective in detecting novel (previously unknown) attacks. *False*

J81   Intrusion detection systems must cope with false positives and false negatives. *True*

J82   Host-based IDS does not perform network traffic analysis. *True*

J83   IDS (Intrusion Detection System) can be implemented as part of firewalls. *True*

J84   Host-based IDSs (HIDSs) cannot detect both external and internal intrusions. *False*

J85   NIDS (Network-based Intrusion Detection System) analyzes only network layer traffic, but not application layer traffic. *False*

J86   NIDS analyzes transport layer traffic, in addition to network layer traffic. *True*

J87   The deviations in the behavior of an intruder from that of a legitimate user cannot be quantified. *False*

J88   An inline sensor monitors the actual network traffic passing through the device. _**True**_

J89   A common location for a NIDS sensor is just inside the external firewall. _**True**_

J90   Network-based intrusion detection uses anomaly detection, but not signature detection. _**False**_

J91   Network-based intrusion detection uses both anomaly detection and signature detection. _**True**_

J92   Host-based intrusion detection uses signature detection, but not anomaly detection. _**False**_

J93   An Intrusion Prevention System detects bad packets, but will not block them. _**False**_

J94   A host-based IPS uses either signature detection technique or anomaly detection technique, but not both. _**False**_

J95   Anomaly detection is effective against misfeasors. _**False**_

J96   Anomaly-based intrusion detection system (IDS) will never miss known attacks. _**False**_

J97   Signature-based detection has the ability to potentially detect novel attacks. _**False**_

IOIOIOIOIOIOIOIOIOIOIOIOIOIOIOIOIOIOIOIOIOIOIOIOIOIOIOIOIOI

Answers
(Sentence Completion)

A. Overview

A1   A weakness in the security of a system that may be exploited is known as *__vulnerability__*.

A2   A set of circumstances that may allow a vulnerability to be exploited is known as *__threat__*.

A3   When both vulnerability and threat exist, then *__risk__* exists.

A4   Reducing the damage due to an attack is known as *__mitigation__*.

A5   Technique to make the attacks harder is known as *__deterrence__*.

A6   Technique to make the current target less attractive is known as *__deflection__*.

A7   Getting the system back in action after an attack is known as *__recovery__*.

A8   Methods to handle attacks on a computer/network are known as *__controls__*.

A9   Use of methods/techniques intended to break encryption is known as *__cryptanalysis__*.

A10   Cryptography and cryptanalysis are together known as *__cryptology__*.

A11   The three main aspects/goals of computer/network security are: *__confidentiality__*, *__integrity__*, and *__availability__*.

A12   The three necessary ingredients before planning an attack are *__method__*, *__opportunity__*, and *__motive__*.

A13   Verifying that the subject is authorized to perform the operation on an object is called *__mediation__*.

A14   The components of *access control* are *__authentication__*, *__authorization__*, and *__auditing__*.

A15   Provision of *confidentiality* protects data from getting disclosed to unauthorized users.

A16   Provision of *integrity* protects data from modification by unauthorized users.

A17   Provision of *nonrepudiation* protects against denial of sending/receiving messages.

A18   Example authenticator(s) that a person *knows* are *passwords, personal identification numbers (PINs), etc*.

A19   Example authenticator(s) that a person *has* (possesses) are *electronic access cards, smart cards, etc*.

A20   Example authenticator(s) that a person *is* are *fingerprint, retina, etc*.

A21   Example authenticator(s) that a person *does* are *voice pattern, handwriting,* etc.

A22   *Availability* refers to reliable and timely access to data and resources provided to authorized individuals.

A23   The hardware, software, and firmware that provide some type of security protection are the components of *trusted computing base (TCB)*.

A24   An imaginary boundary that has trusted components (that make up the TCB) within it and untrusted components outside it is known as *security perimeter*.

A25   The components of the CIA triad in security are *confidentiality, integrity*, and *availability*.

A26   Hiding data within other files/images is *steganography*.

A27   Masking of data in order to create data that is structurally similar to original data but is not authentic is known as *data obfuscation*.

A28   Monitoring and keeping records of user accesses to system resources is known as *auditing*.

A29 **_Authentication_** is the process of verification of the validity credentials of a user / entity.

A30 **_Authorization_** is the process of granting of rights (permissions) to a user / entity to access system resource(s).

A31 Unauthorized transfer of data from a computer system is known as **_data exfiltration (data extrusion, data exportation)_**.

A32 The _Bell-LaPadula_ model was developed to address **_data confidentiality_** aspect of security.

A33 The _Biba_ model was developed to address **_data integrity_** aspect of security.

A34 The _Clark-Wilson_ model was developed to address **_data integrity_** aspect of security.

A35 The model that requires that all modifications to data and objects be done through programs is the **_Clark-Wilson_** model.

B. Cryptography

B1   The class of techniques/ciphers where the cipher text symbols are the same as plaintext symbols, but are at different positions is called ***transposition*** ciphers.

B2   The non–linearity of the encryption which makes it harder to determine the relationship between the plaintext, key, and ciphertext provides the ***confusion*** property.

B3   The property of the encryption which makes a change in plaintext affect as many parts (bits) of the ciphertext as possible, is known as ***diffusion***.

B4   The number of possible plaintext blocks for a block of size N bits is $\underline{2^N}$.

B5   The key length in DES is **56** bits.

B6   The length of the round key (key used in each round) in DES is **48** bits.

B7   The number of Substitution boxes (S–box) in DES is **8**.

B8   The number of elements in each S–box in DES is **64**.

B9   The elements of S–boxes in DES are in the range **0–15**.

B10   The encryption which works on bit or bytes of the plaintext/input is called ***stream*** cipher.

B11   In public key encryption, for confidentiality, the message is encrypted using ***receiver's public key***.

B12   In public key encryption, for authentication, the message is decrypted using ***sender's public key***.

B13   Number of *S-boxes* used in DES is **8**.

B14   Each *S-box* of DES consists of **4** rows and **16** columns.

B15   The range of values of the elements of an *S-box* of DES is **0 – 15**.

B16   Given that the input template to *S-box* 5 of DES is **1XXXX0** (where X = 0 or 1), and the output is **1011**, the actual input is **100110**.
[The row number is 10 (= 2). The output is 1011 = 11. In S5, the column number in row number 2 with a value of 11 is 3 = 0011. Thus, the input is 100110]

B17   Given that the input template to *S-box* 3 of DES is **X1001X** (where X = 0 or 1), and the output is 0001, the actual input is **110010**.
[Column number = 1001 = 9; Under column number 9, the value 1 (0001) is in row number 2 = 10. Therefore, the input is: 110010]

B18   Given that the input template to *S-box* 5 of DES is **0XXXX1** (where X = 0 or 1), and the output is **1011**, the actual input is **000011**.
[The row number is 01 (= 1). The output is 1011 = 11. In S5, the column number in row number 1 with a value of 11 is 1 = 0001. Thus, the input is 000011]

B19   Given that the input to *S-box* 2 of DES is **010001**, the corresponding output is **1100**
[The value at row number 01 (= 1) and column 1000 (= 8) in S2 is 12 = 1100]

B20   Given that the input template to S-box 7 of DES is **1XXXX1** (where X = 0 or 1), and the output is **1101**, the actual input is **000011**
[The row number is 11 (= 3). The output is 1101 = 13. In S7, the column number in row number 3 with a value of 13 is 2 = 0010. Thus, the input is **100101**]

B21   The number of new keys generated by the *expand key* stage of AES is **10 (1 new key / round)**

B22   The number of rounds in the encryption process of AES is **16**.

B23   The number of rounds in the encryption process of AES is **10**.

B24   The block size of data in AES is **128** bits.

B25   The key sizes of AES are **128, 192, and 156** bits.

B26   In AES, for an original key size of 128 bits, the size of a round key is **128** bits.

B27   In AES encryption, the number of rounds of processing for 128-bit keys is **10**, for 192-bit keys it is **12**, and for 256-bit keys it is **14**.

B28   In the substitute byte stage of AES, the output for an input byte of value 6B is **7F**. (Value at row number 6 and column number B of the S–Box)

B29   In the Substitute Byte stage of AES, if the output byte is 4E, the input byte value is **B6**

B30   In the *forward shift row* stage of AES, if row 3 of the (4 x 4 byte) input is 4A C3 46 E7, the corresponding output (row 3 of the 4 x 4 byte) is **E7 4A C3 46**

B31   In the *add round key* stage of AES, if a byte of input is 94, and the corresponding byte of the round key is 66, the corresponding output is **F2 = 94 $\oplus$ 66**

B32   Using public-key system, to ensure message *confidentiality* it should be encrypted using by the receiver's ***public*** key.

B33   In the ***Electronic Code Book (ECB)*** mode of DES an error in block number *i* of the ciphertext during storage/transmission affects only plaintext block ***i*** at the decoder.

B34   In the **ECB (*Electronic Code Book*)** mode of DES decryption of any block of ciphertext is independent on any other ciphertext block(s).

B35   In the CBC (Cipher Block Chaining) mode of DES, an error in block 3 (C_3) of the ciphertext would affect only plaintext blocks **3 (P_3)** and **4 (P_4)** at the decoder.

B36   In the ***Cipher Block Chaining* (CBC)** mode of DES, an error in a block i of ciphertext would affect only plaintext blocks i and $i + 1$ at the decoder.

B37   In the CFB (Cipher Feed Back) mode of DES, an error in block number 3 of the ciphertext during its transmission to the decoder would affect blocks **3, 4, 5, ... etc.** of plaintext produced at the decoder.

B38   In the ***Cipher Feed back (CFB)*** mode of DES, an error in a block of ciphertext during storage/transmission would affect all subsequent plaintext blocks produced at the decoder.

B39   In the CBC (Cipher Block Chaining*)* mode of DES, the cipher text output C_i of the ith stage of encoder (with encoding function E_K) is $C_i = \mathbf{E_K} [P_i \oplus C_{i-1}]$.

B40   In the CBC (Cipher Block Chaining*)* mode of DES, the plaintext output P_i of the ith stage of decoder (with encoding function D_K) is $P_i = \mathbf{D_K} [C_i] \oplus C_{i-1}$.

B41   ***RSA*** is a block cipher in which the plaintext and ciphertext are both (treated as) integers between 0 and $N-1$ for some N.

B42   In the encryption using the *RSA algorithm*, given the two prime numbers to be $p = 3$ and $q = 11$, chosen (part of) public key $e = 3$, and plaintext message $M = 5$,

    i. the value of n (part of private/public) key is $n = pq = 3 * 11 = 33$

    ii. the value of Euler totient function $\phi(n)$ is $\phi(n) = (p - 1)(q - 1) = 2 * 10 = 20$

    iii. the computed value of (part of) private key d is $d = e^{-1} MOD\ \phi(n)$ $\rightarrow d = 7$

    iv. the cipher-text C is $C = M^e$ MOD $n = 5^3$ MOD 33 = 125 MOD 33 = 26

B43   Given that the *last row* of the state matrix of AES is **16 3E A7 8F**, the values after it goes through the *shift rows* stage of AES is **8F 16 3E A7**.

B44   In the Substitute Byte stage of AES, the output for an input byte of value 6B is **7F** (value in row number 6 and column number B of the *S*–Box).

B45   Given that a byte of the state matrix is 1C, and assuming AE to be the corresponding byte of the key, its value after it goes through the *AddRoundKey* stage of AES, will be **B2** [1C = 0001 1100; AE = 1010 1110; After bitwise $\oplus$ (XOR), we get 1011 0010 = B2]

B46   The security of Triple DES is **2** times the security of DES.

B47   The two types of *symmetric* ciphers are ***block*** ciphers and ***stream*** ciphers.

B48   The direct use of DES is known as ***electronic code book (ECB)*** mode.

B49   In the ***cipher block chaining (CBC)*** mode of DES, the ciphertext depends on the input plaintext block as well as the preceding ciphertext block.

B50   To send an encrypted message using public-key cryptography, the message is encrypted using receiver's ***public*** key.

B51   Using public-key cryptography, the sender can assure the receiver that the message indeed came from that sender by encrypting the message using sender's ***private*** key.

B52   In public-key cryptography, message confidentiality is provided by encrypting the message using ***public*** key of ***receiver***.

B53   In public-key cryptography, message authentication is provided by encryption using ***private*** key of ***sender***.

B54   The technique that disperses the statistical structure of plaintext over the ciphertext is known as ***diffusion***.

B55   The technique which hides the relationship between ciphertext and secret key is known as *confusion*.

B56   A small change in plaintext resulting in a considerable change in the ciphertext is known as *avalanche effect*.

B57   Any block cipher can be converted into a stream cipher by using the *Cipher Feedback (CFB)* mode.

B58   In the CBC mode of DES, the input to the encryption algorithm consists of the XOR of *the plaintext block* and *the ciphertext of the previous plaintext block*.

B59   In the *CBC* mode of DES, the ciphertext block for any given plaintext block is a function of all the previous ciphertext blocks.

B60   In (almost all) stream ciphers, the encryption operation (function) used is *XOR*.

B61   In (almost all) stream ciphers, the ciphertext (byte) is computed by applying the *XOR* function to the *plaintext* (byte) and *pseudorandom key stream* (byte).

B62   In (almost all) stream ciphers, the pseudorandom key (byte) stream is function of *the encryption key*.

B63   *Stream* ciphers are used in short data transfers between Web servers and browsers.

B64   *Block* ciphers are commonly used in file transfers.

B65   The scheme of a symmetric block cipher structure which uses the same algorithm for both encryption and decryption, and which is the basis of numerous symmetric key cipher systems, including DES, is known as *Feistel cipher (network)*.

B66   The block size of plaintext handled by 3DES is **64 bits**.

B67   Repeated application of DES to blocks formed by the XOR of the current plaintext block and the preceding ciphertext block is known as *cipher block chaining* mode.

B68 Confusion is commonly carried out through _**substitution**_.

B69 _**Diffusion**_ is carried out by using transposition.

B70 _**Diffusion**_ is the transposition processes used in encryption functions to increase randomness.

B71 _**Confusion**_ is the substitution processes used in encryption functions to increase randomness.

B72 Making each bit of the key affect as many bits of the ciphertext block as possible, is known as _**confusion**_.

B73 The goal of the substitution performed by an S-box of DES is to enhance _**diffusion**_.

B74 Use of _**initialization vectors (IVs)**_ ensures that two identical plaintext values that are encrypted with the same key will not result in the same ciphertext.

B75 The cipher which uses more than one alphabet to thwart frequency analysis is known as _**polyalphabetic cipher**_.

B76 In AES, an inverse function is used in the decryption algorithm for the _**Substitute Byte**_, _**Shift Row**_, and _**Mix Columns**_ stages of the encryption algorithm.

B77 In AES, only the _**Add Round Key**_ stage makes use of the key.

B78 In an AES round, the most computation (complex operation) is performed in the _**Mix Columns**_ stage.

B79 In an AES round, the operation required in substitute byte transformation is (just a) _**table lookup**_.

B80 In AES, the substitution box (S-box) is a table of **16** rows and **16** columns, and each element is of size **8 bits (1 byte)**.

B81 The values in the S-Box and Inverse S-Box of AES are in the range **00** to **FF**.

B82   The difficulty of breaking the RSA encryption is based on the difficulty of computation of **_prime factors (of large numbers)_**.

B83   The difficulty of breaking the *Diffie–Hellman* encryption is based on the difficulty of computation of **_discrete logarithm_**.

B84   In a public-key system, encryption with the **_private_** key of **_sender_** provides authentication.

B85   In a public–key system, encryption with the **_public_** key of **_receiver_** provides confidentiality.

B86   The **_CFB_** and **_OFB_** modes of DES mimic (simulate) the stream cipher.

B87   The period of the Pseudorandom Byte sequence in RC4 is $\sim 10^{100}$

B88   The key size of elliptic-curve cryptography (ECC) is (smaller?/larger?) **_smaller_** than that of RSA (for the same security strength).

B89   In public-key cryptosystem, it is computationally infeasible to compute the **_private_** key with a knowledge of the **_public_** key.

B90   Encrypted data that is produced by encrypting a bit (or byte) of data at a time is known as **_stream cipher_**.

B91   When the ciphertext gives absolutely no additional information about the plaintext, it is known as **_perfect secrecy_**.

B92   The essential operation done in the 'shift rows' step of Advanced Encryption Standard (AES) is **_permutation_**.

B93   The stage of symmetric key encryption where each element in the plaintext is mapped into another element, is known as **_substitution_**.

B94   The stage of symmetric key encryption where each element in the plaintext is rearranged (positionally), is known as **_transposition_**.

B95   In a symmetric key cryptosystem using a key of N bits, the number of possible keys to be tried on average in a brute-force attack is $\mathbf{2^N/2 = 2^{N-1}}$.

B96   In a symmetric key cryptosystem, if the key length is increased by 4 bits, the effort required to break in a brute-force attack is increased by a factor of $\mathbf{2^4 = 16}$.

B97   Random values, at least as long as the message itself, that are XORed with the message to produce ciphertext, and then discarded is known as ***onetime pad***.

B98   The condition where that two different keys generate the same ciphertext for the same message is known as ***key clustering***.

B99   A function that is easy to compute in one direction (given x, to compute $f(x)$), but extremely difficult to do inverse computation (given $f(x)$, to compute x) is known as ***one-way function***.

B100   A one-way function which makes it easier to do the inverse computation given some additional (extra) information is known as ***one-way trapdoor***.

C. Key Generation, Distribution, and Management

C1 For *connectionless* protocols, a new session key is used for each message exchange.

C2 The "number" which is used one-time during authentication / key exchange / key distribution is called *nonce*.

C3 The KDC in each of the domains in hierarchical key control is called *local KDC*

C4 In *decentralized* key control, it is possible for the users to exchange session keys without the KDC.

C5 Public key encryption is commonly used to encrypt *keys* but not data.

C6 Number of keys required in the node-level encryption of 100 nodes is $99*50 = 4950$

C7 Number of master keys shared between 100 hosts and a KDC (Key Distribution Center) is **100**

C8 In hierarchical key control, each of the domains will have a *local* KDC.

C9 The number of session keys required for pairwise communication among N users using the Key Distribution Center (KDC) for the generation and distribution of session keys is $N(N-1)/2$.

C10 The number of messages required for session keys distribution and mutual authentication between two users, using the Key Distribution Center (KDC) is **5**.

C11 Using the Key Distribution Center (KDC), the number of messages required for the distribution of session keys and for mutual authentication between a pair of users, for N users is $5N(N-1)/2$.

C12   In public-key cryptography, for secure pairwise communication among N users, the number of distinct private-public key pairs required is __N__.

C13   In symmetric-key cryptography, for secure pairwise communication among N users, the number of distinct keys required is __$N(N-1)/2$__.

C14   The *Diffie–Hellman* scheme provides the functionality of ___key exchange___.

C15   Use of ___public key certificate___ reduces the traffic to public–key authority.

C16   The Digital Signature (is very simply), encryption of the ___message digest___ using ___sender's private key___.

C17   In the public–key distribution using key authority, the key distribution takes **5 (7 w/auth)_steps**.

C18   Session keys are derived from ___long-term keys___.

C19   Personal computers and laptops come pre-loaded with the public keys of ___the root CAs___.

C20   ___Trusted Platform Module (TPM)___ chip is a hardware chip that stores encryption keys.

C21   Diffie-Hellman scheme is a method for secure exchange of ___secret___ keys.

C22   Internet Security Association and Key Management Protocol (ISAKMP) provides a framework for ___security association creation___ and ___key exchange___.

C23   ___Internet Key Exchange (IKE)___ provides authenticated keying material for use with the Internet Security Association and Key Management Protocol (ISAKMP).

D. Authentication, Hash Functions, Digital Signatures / Certificates

D1   One-way hash function is also known as **_secure hash function_**.

D2   Each stage of the SHA–1 (Secure Hash Algorithm) takes input of **512** bits.

D3   The final output of SHA–1 after working on the entire input is **160** bits.

D4   The output of a Hash function, the hash value, is called a **_message digest_**.

D5   The property of a cryptographic hash function where it is not computationally feasible to find two distinct inputs having the same hash value is called **_collision resistance_**.

D6   The property of a hash function H such that, it is computationally infeasible to find any pair (x, y) with $H(x) = H(y)$ is known as **_strong collision resistance_**.

D7   The property of a hash function H such that, it is computationally infeasible to find $y \neq x$ with $H(y) = H(x)$ is known as **_weak collision resistance_**.

D8   Use of authentication information within a trusted group of systems after positive identification of a user (without multiple logins) is known as **_single sign-on_**.

D9   The condition where two (or more) distinct messages have the same message digest is known as **_collision_**.

D10   The number of possible hash codes of length b bits is **2^b**.

D11   The probability of a message not being hashed to a given hash code h among N equally probable hash codes, is $\left(1 - \dfrac{1}{N}\right)$

D12   The probability of two arbitrary messages not being hashed to a given hash code h among N equally probable hash codes, is $\left(1 - \frac{1}{N}\right)^2$

D13   Among k random messages, the probability that none of the messages is hashed to a given hash code h among N equally probable hash codes, is $\left(1 - \frac{1}{N}\right)^k$

D14   Among k random messages, the probability that at least one of the messages is hashed to a given hash code h among N equally probable hash codes, is $1 - \left(1 - \frac{1}{N}\right)^k$

D15   Among k random messages, the probability that at least one pair of messages which hashes to a given hash code h among N equally probable hash codes, is $1 - \frac{N!}{(N-k)!N^k}$

D16   Message digests are used to ensure ***integrity*** of messages.

D17   A message authentication code (MAC) is also known as ***cryptographic checksum***.

D18   Use of ***public key certificate*** reduces the traffic to Public-key authority.

D19   Public key certificate is verified using the ***public*** key of ***the certification authority***.

D20   The list of digital certificates whose corresponding private keys are believed to have been compromised or lost is known as ***certificate revocation list***.

D21   The chain of certificates associated with a given digital certificate is known as ***chain of trust***.

D22   A self-signed certificate is also known as ***root certificate***.

D23   The digital certificate of the certificate authority is known as ***root certificate***.

D24   The public key of a user (system) that is digitally signed by a trusted third party is known as ***digital certificate***.

D25   Certifying the ownership of a public key is done using ***digital certificates***.

D26   The entity issuing the digital certificates is known as ***certificate authority (CA)***.

D27   SHA-l has a message digest of **160** bits.

D28   Requiring two pieces of information for authentication of a claimed identity is known as ***two-factor authentication***.

D29   Number of messages required per user to get a public key certificate from certificate authority is **2**.

D30   Number of messages required for mutual authentication for a pair of users is **2**.

D31   Total number of messages required for pair-wise mutual authentication of 100 users is **2 (100 x 99 / 2) = 9,900**.

D32   Centrally authenticating multiple systems and applications against a federated user database is ***single sign-on***.

D33   While sending messages to multiple users, use of ***digital signature*** is better (more efficient) than ***MACs*** for authentication.

D34   Nonrepudiation without employing a trusted third party is possible by the use of ***digital signatures***.

D35   Data integrity is ensured for data sent between two IPsec-enabled hosts by using ***message digests***.

D36   In practice, the ***message digest*** is signed instead of the original message.

D37   In the generation of message authentication codes (MACs), only the ***encryption key*** is kept secret.

D38   The certification authority (CA) knows only the **public** key of a user.

D39   The recipient of a digitally signed message needs to use the **public** key of the sender to verify the digital signature.

D40   Generation of a digital signature requires the **private** key of the sender.

D41   **X.509** certificates are used in IPSec, SSL (secure sockets layer), and SET (secure electronic transactions).

D42   The most widely used format for public-key certificates is **X.509**.

D43   **Serial number** is a unique integer value within the issuing CA that is unambiguously associated with the certificate.

D44   A system that stores the passwords of all users in centralized database and confirms the identities of users requesting services is known as **authentication server (AS)**.

D45   The model upon which most remote authentication systems (both public domain and commercial products) are based is **Kerberos**.

D46   **Trusted Platform Module (TPM)** chip is used for hardware authentication.

D47   The PKI implementation element is responsible for verifying the authenticity of certificate contents is **certification authority (CA)**.

D48   The digital certificate is signed by the certificate authority's **private** key.

D49   Decrypting the hash of an electronic signature is done using the **public key**.

D50   Unified use of separate identification and authentication systems is known as **federated identity management**.

D51   Combining information from multiple forms of authentication is known as **multifactor authentication**.

D52   The size of the hash code produced by SHA–1 for a message input of size 32 Kbytes is **160 bits** (It does not depend on the message size).

D53   The hash algorithm used in digital signature standard (DSS) is ***SHA-1***.

D54   The signature of a digitally signed digital certificate is verifies using the ***public*** key of ***the certification authority***.

D55   The digital certificate is essentially the ***public*** key of an entity signed using the ***private*** key of ***the certification authority***.

D56   Digital certificates facilitate secure sharing of ***public*** keys.

D57   Pre-authentication of users before actually grating service to desired services is done by ***bastion*** hosts.

D58   ***Authentication server*** could be considered a single point of failure in *single sign-on* system.

D59   A trusted third party that holds their public keys of users and generates and maintains user certificates, is known as ***certificate authority (CA)***.

D60   The number of bits in the hash value produced by SHA-1 (used in DSS) is **160**.

D61   Verification of the identification information (username/password, etc.) is known as ***authentication***.

D62   A portable identity that can be used across business boundaries allowing a user to be authenticated across multiple IT systems and enterprises is known as ***federated identity***.

D63   Allowing a user to enter credentials one time and be able to access all pre-authorized resources in primary and secondary network domains is known as ***single sign-on***.

D64   Most Internet service providers (ISPs) use ***RADIUS*** to authenticate customers before allowing access to the Internet.

D65 Kerberos is based upon the *Needham-Schroeder* protocol.

D66 The common protocol schematic used for remote user authentication is known as *challenge-response* protocol.

D67 The two broad steps used in an authentication process are *identification* and *verification*.

D68 A graphical puzzle used as an attempt to distinguish input of human users from automated (software) agents is known as *CAPTCHA* (completely automated public Turing test to tell computers and humans apart).

D69 A type of challenge–response test used to determine whether or not the input/interaction is from a human user is known as *CAPTCHA*.

D70 DSS is used only for *digital signatures*.

D71 Some form of *challenge-response* protocol is commonly used for remote user authentication.

D72 Adding random strings to passwords before encrypting and saving them is known as *password salting*.

D73 Adding extra data to passwords so that identical passwords have different encrypted values (under the same encryption) is known as *salting*.

D74 Use of *salt* together with password increases the protection to dictionary attacks.

D75 A randomly chosen bit pattern that is combined with the actual password, before it is hashed and stored, is known as *salt*.

D76 The file containing hashed passwords that is kept separately from the user IDs, is known as *shadow password file*.

D77 The table containing pre-calculated hashes of all passwords available within a certain character space is known as *rainbow table*.

D78   The **_synchronous token_** device synchronizes with the authentication service by using internal time or events.

E. Software and Operating Systems Security

E1   An undocumented access point is called **_trap door_**.

E2   The arguments, return address, and the stack pointer corresponding to a function call, stored on stack is together called **_stack frame_**.

E3   Passing more arguments than expected to a function, which goes unchecked, could cause **_stack overflow_**.

E4   The registers used by OS to ensure that the users' programs stay within their permitted memory space are **_base_** and **_bounds_** registers.

E5   The component of an operating system that regulates the access by subjects to objects based on security parameters is known as **_reference monitor_**.

E6   The part of the OS consisting of the fundamental and primitive operations is known as **_kernel_**.

E7   *Reference monitor* is the component of an operating system that regulates the access to **_objects_** by **_subjects_** based on **_security parameters_**.

E8   The architecture where every word of memory has extra bits to identify access rights to it is known as **_tagged_** architecture.

E9   The way in which a subject may access an object is specified by **_access rights_**.

E10   The security practice that is part of initial software development is **_secure code review_**.

E11   Penetration testing performed by security professionals with limited inside knowledge of the network is **_gray box_** testing.

E12 The layer of the operating system which intercepts all requests to use of resources is known as ***reference monitor***.

E13 The part of the operating system that handles all security related issues is known as ***security kernel***.

E14 The OS protection mechanism that mediates all access that subjects have to objects to ensure that the subjects have the necessary rights to access the objects is ***reference monitor***.

E15 The part of operating system kernel that is invoked each time a subject makes a request to access an object, and enforces the access rules is known as ***reference monitor***.

E16 Use of a collection of tools, techniques, and best practices to reduce vulnerability in systems is known as ***systems hardening***.

E17 Adding protection mechanisms to programs/software to make it hard for attackers to exploit is known as ***software hardening***.

E18 Technologies used to specify which applications are authorized for use on a host are known as ***application whitelisting***.

E19 A controlled environment that restricts the operations that applications can perform and that isolates applications running on the same host is known as ***sandboxing***.

E20 Code (software) that is transmitted across a network, to be executed by a (remote) system or device on the other end, is known as ***mobile code***.

E21 A virtual environment that allows for fine-grained control over the actions of code within a machine is known as ***sandbox***.

E22 A virtual environment that allows safe execution of untrusted code from remote sources is known as ***sandbox***.

E23 Giving programs and users nothing more than the minimal amount of privilege needed to function correctly, is known as ***the principle of least privilege***.

E24   List containing the mapping of users to access rights of resources is known as ***access control list (ACL)***.

E25   A framework that specifies how subjects access objects is known as ***access control model***.

E26   Reference monitor is enforced by the ***security kernel*** part of the operating system.

E27   Every access request of a subject for an object, the rules of the access control model are checked by the ***security kernel***.

E28   To determine if the request of a subject for an object is allowed is determined by the rules specified in the ***access control model***.

E29   Users are not allowed to determine the access of objects by subjects in the ***mandatory access control (MAC)*** model.

E30   In the *mandatory access control (MAC)* model, the access/security policy is enforced by ***the operating system***.

E31   A centrally administrated set of controls to determine how subjects and objects interact is used in the ***role-based access control (RBAC)*** model.

E32   *Rule-based* access control which uses specific rules indicating the access rights of subjects to objects is an access control (technology / policy) ***technology***.

E33   ***Database views*** are mechanisms used to restrict access by users to data contained in databases.

E34   ***Access control list*** is bound to an object and indicates the set of subjects that can access the object and the operations they can perform.

E35   ***Capability table*** is bound to a subject and indicates the set of objects that the subject can access and the operations it can perform.

E36   A matrix of subjects (usually in rows) and objects (usually in columns) and the entries containing access rights is known as *access control matrix*.

E37   In *content-dependent* access control, access to objects is determined by the content within the object.

E38   Extra spaces inserted between critical regions in the address space of a processes to prevent buffer overflow attacks, are known as *guard pages*.

E39   The process of designing and implementing software so that it continues to function even when under attack is known as *defensive (secure) programming*.

E40   A *multilevel* security system processes data at different classifications (security levels), and supports users with different clearances (security levels).

E41   The facility used during software development which enables code to be executed without the usual security checks is known as *maintenance hook*.

E42   Legitimate backdoors used by programmers to debug and test programs are known as *maintenance hooks*.

E43   Organizing subjects in rows and objects in columns and the cells containing access rights in a matrix, is known as *access control matrix*.

E44   Use of rules and criteria to make a determination of operations that a subject can carry out on objects is known as *authorization*.

E45   Reviewing a piece of code without actually running it is called *static analysis*.

E46   Actually running the code, observing, and studying the behavior is called *dynamic analysis*.

E47   The technique of providing invalid, unexpected, or random data as input to a program is known as *fuzz testing* or *fuzzing*.

E48   Software testing technique that uses large amounts of randomly generated data as inputs to a program to determine its robustness is known as *(input) fuzzing*.

E49   Feeding a target system with automatically generated malformed data designed to trigger implementation flaws is known as *fuzzing*.

E50   Access control is usually performed by *the operating system*.

E51   The most common phase during which backdoors are inserted is *application development*.

E52   *Capabilities* allow a user to pass a permission to another user.

E53   In the context of access control, possession of data which proves authorization to access a resource is known as a *capability*.

E54   *Access control lists* make it easier to revoke a specific permission of a specific user.

E55   The *discretionary* access control model is user-directed.

E56   The rules specifying which subjects can access specific resources can be set by the owner of the resources in the *discretionary* access control model.

E57   Methodical probing of the target in order to identify weaknesses is known as *penetration testing*.

E58   The two control policies used to protect relational databases are *mandatory access control (MAC)* and *discretionary access control (DAC)*.

E59   *Open Vulnerability and Assessment Language (OVAL)* is a standard for representing vulnerability information.

E60   A non-malicious attack against a network that is intended to test the security measures in place is known as *penetration test*.

E61   Access control technologies commonly used to protect copyright material is known as *digital rights management (DRM)*.

E62   A less-secure channel via which the data written to storage is allowed to be read, is known as ***covert storage channel***.

F. Malware

F1   *Stealth* virus hides signs that it has infected the system.

F2   *Stealth* virus has the capability to hide from operating system or anti-virus software.

F3   *Stealth* virus has the capability to hide by making changes to file sizes or directory structure.

F4   *Retrovirus* is a type virus which tries to attack and disable the anti-virus application running on the computer.

F5   *Polymorphic* virus changes its appearance.

F6   *Polymorphic* virus usually changes signature upon replication.

F7   *Polymorphic* virus is capable of changing its code every time it infects a different system.

F8   Example(s) of source code / text file that could be infected by viruses is/are *macros*, *scripts*.

F9   The typical phases in the lifetime of a typical virus are *dormant*, *propagation*, *triggering*, and *execution*.

F10   The actual function of the virus is performed in the *execution* phase.

F11   The *multipartite* virus can affect both the boot sector and the program files at the same time.

F12   The functionality of virus remains same but its signature is changed in a *polymorphic* virus.

F13   Malicious code installed in the most privileged part (root) of the operating system is known as *rootkit*.

F14   A collection of tools used by a malicious user to mask intrusion and gain administrative-level access to a computer is known as *rootkit*.

F15 **_Rootkits_** conceal malware and/or prevent malicious programs being detected.

F16 Boot sector virus infects the **_master boot record_**.

F17 A legitimate file with a masked virus is known as **_Trojan horse_**.

F18 The most common method of virus propagation is **_via email_**.

F19 A special type of polymorphic virus that completely rewrites itself periodically is known as **_metamorphic_** virus.

F20 The virus which performs its malicious activity sporadically is known as **_sparse virus_**.

F21 The virus that attacks the computer in multiple ways is known as **_multi-partite_** virus.

F22 The software that records activities on the computer are known as **_spyware_**.

F23 The most common way for a spyware to get into a computer is via **_Trojan horse_**.

F24 **_Spyware_** is software that communicates information from a user's system to a malicious entity without knowledge of the user.

F25 **_Trojans_** are malicious programs disguised as useful applications.

F26 The stage/phase when the virus is idle is known as **_dormant phase_**.

F27 The stage/phase when the virus function is performed is known as **_execution phase_**.

F28 The stage/phase when the virus is multiplying and replicating itself is known as **_propagation phase_**.

F29 The stage/phase when the virus is activated to perform its intended function is known as **_triggering phase_**.

F30 The attack that uses multiple methods of infection and/or propagation is known as **_blended attack_**.

F31   The malware used to capture keystrokes on the infected machine to gather sensitive information is known as **_keylogger_**.

F32   Virus that stays in memory (RAM) all the time, is known as **_memory-resident_** virus.

F33   Malware which encrypts user's data, and demands payment in exchange for the key needed to recover the data is known as **_ransomware_**.

F34   **_Polymorphic_** viruses vary the sequence of their instructions by including bogus instructions with other useful instructions.

F35   A **_polymorphic_** virus has the capability to change its own code.

F36   In the context of virus detection, *signature-based* detection also called **_fingerprint_** detection.

F37   The technique that analyzes the overall structure of the malicious code, evaluates the coded instructions and logic functions is known as **_heuristic_** detection.

F38   Hidden entry points in a system that are set to bypass security measures are known as **_trap-doors_**.

F39   Part of a virus that helps in performing malicious activities is the **_payload_**.

F40   Software that records the keystrokes on a keyboard is called **_keylogger_**.

F41   A virus usually attaches to **_executable_** files and propagates.

F42   The virus scanning that uses complex rules to define what is / is not a virus is known as **_heuristic_** scanning.

F43   File with a list of known viruses, their sizes, properties, and behavior is known as **_virus definition file_**.

F44   Antivirus programs will be most effective when **_virus definition_** files are kept up-to-date.

F45   The most commonly used technical control for malware threat mitigation is ***antivirus software***.

F46   The kind of virus that changes its own code, making it harder to detect with antivirus software is known as ***polymorphic virus***.

F47   The most common way for a virus scanner to recognize a virus is look for known virus attributes in the ***virus definition file***.

F48   Comparing executable files with bit patterns of known viruses is known as ***signature scan***.

F49   Antivirus signatures are essentially ***hashes***.

F50   Virus scanners look for ***signature*** which are associated with some pattern(s) associated with a virus.

G. Attacks

G1   Use of random numbers in the authentication process defends against *__replay__* attacks.

G2   Capturing packets, and then placing packets back on the network is known as *__replay__* attack.

G3   A form of social engineering where an intruder pretends as a legitimate user and gathers sensitive information from (gullible) users is known as *__phishing__*.

G4   A security threat where an attacker falsifies the IP address of a server in the packet header is known as *__spoofing__*.

G5   Attempt at breaking passwords by (automatically) trying every word in the dictionary, encrypting and comparing with stored passwords is known as *__dictionary__* attack.

G6   A threat (attack) combining the characteristics of several attacks such as a virus, worm, Trojans, etc., is known as *__blended threat__*.

G7   The attack where the user is tricked into revealing sensitive information or taking unsafe action, is known as *__phishing__* attack.

G8   A process for preventing session creation through a particular port is known as *__port knocking__*.

G9   A bot server or controller together with one or more client-bots is known as *__botnet__*.

G10   The infected computers in the botnet connection are called *__zombies__*.

G11   The attack which overwhelms the server with a surge of requests more than the server can handle is known as *__denial of service (DoS)__* attack.

G12   A DoS attack coming from a large number of IP addresses is known as *__distributed denial of service (DDoS)__* attack.

G13   UDP flooding is an attack on the *availability* aspect of security.

G14   Monitoring (and capturing) data packets passing through a target network is known as *sniffing*.

G15   Sniffing involves data (interception? / interruption?) *interception*.

G16   The most commonly used session hijacking attack is *IP spoofing*.

G17   Attack where malicious code/script is injected into a Web application (Web page) using vulnerability in a Web site is known as *cross-site scripting (XSS)*.

G18   DNS cache poisoning is also known as *DNS spoofing*.

G19   The attack which uses DNS vulnerabilities for diverting the traffic away from genuine servers is known as *DNS spoofing*.

G20   *ICMP* should be blocked at the network perimeter to prevent host enumeration by sweep devices.

G21   *Address resolution protocol (ARP) poisoning* results in incorrect hardware (MAC) addresses corresponding to IP addresses.

G22   Attack using the vulnerability that has been found but not yet known to the application creator/owner is known as *zero-day exploit*.

G23   Vulnerability that has been identified for which there is no known fix yet, is known as *zero-day vulnerability*.

G24   Getting several Internet routers to attack a target server/system is known as *distributed reflection DoS* attack.

G25   In the distributed reflection DoS attack, connection requests are sent to several routers such that they have the IP address of *the target/victim system*.

G26   SYN flood attack is a form of *denial of service (DoS)* attack.

G27   The Smurf attack is a form of *denial of service (DoS)* attack.

G28   Sending fragmented messages in a way which makes it impossible to reassemble them without destroying the individual packet headers is known as **_teardrop_** attack.

G29   A DoS attack that is launched simultaneously from several machines is known as **_distributed denial of service (DDoS)_** attack.

G30   Systematic probing of ports to determine which ones are open is known as **_port scanning_**.

G31   Checking to see if a system is vulnerable to specific attack(s) is known as **_vulnerability assessment_**.

G32   Passing (undesired) Structured Query Language (SQL) commands and making a web site to execute them is known as **_SQL script injection_**.

G33   A bad web site sending innocent victim a script that steals information from a good web site is known as **_cross-site scripting_**.

G34   An attack which modifies the cookie file is called **_cookie poisoning_**.

G35   Unauthorized access of information from a Bluetooth device is known as **_Bluesnarfing_**.

G36   Attack where attacker's MAC address is substituted for victim's MAC address is known as **_ARP poisoning (ARP cache poisoning)_**.

G37   The sequence numbers used in packets thwart the **_replay_** attack.

G38   Nonces are often used to prevent the **_playback (or replay)_** attack.

G39   Time stamps / counters are often used to prevent the **_playback (or replay)_** attack.

G40   Replay attacks are prevented by the use of **_nonces / counters / timestamps_**.

G41   Man-in-the-middle attack is prevented by the use of **_public-key certificates_**.

G42   Modifying the DNS server entry such that connection requests are redirected to the attacker posing as trusted host is known as **_DNS spoofing_**.

G43   Sending an email using a different name in the sender field, impersonating a legitimate user is known as **_email spoofing_**.

G44   Attack using a script inserted in the cookie file is known as **_poison cookie_** attack.

G45   SYN flood attack exploits the **_handshake_** part of the TCP protocol.

G46   **_Teardrop_** attack exploits the IP sequencing/reassembly part of the TCP protocol.

G47   Sending a number of connection requests in excess of that a system can handle is known as **_SYN flood_** attack.

G48   Malware that is dormant until a particular date/time is known as **_time bomb_**.

G49   Malware that triggers action when a predetermined condition occurs is known as **_logic bomb_**.

G50   The **_teardrop_** attack sends a series of IP packet fragments with confusing offsets.

G51   The attack where port 80 is overwhelmed with reload requests is known as **_URL flood attack_**.

G52   DNS server resolves a host name into an incorrect IP address in the **_DNS poisoning_** attack.

G53   Associating the attacker's host MAC (Media Access Control) address with the IP address of a target (legitimate) host is done in **_ARP spoofing_** attack.

G54   Improper (attacker's) IP address is associated with a genuine domain name in the **_DNS poisoning_** attack.

G55   Determining the operating system (OS) that is running on a remote computer is known as *OS fingerprinting*.

G56   MAC Address spoofing is a vulnerability at the *data-link* layer.

G57   IP Address spoofing is a vulnerability at the *network* layer.

G58   In a *DDoS* attack using zombie computers, each of the computers is usually remotely controlled by the attacker.

G59   An attack where numerous SYN packets with spoofed (fake) source addresses are to a server is known as *SYN flood attack*.

G60   In a *SYN flood* attack, the ACK packet is never sent back to the server if the spoofed source address is non-existent.

G61   DNS protocol attack is done in the *application* layer of the TCP/IP model.

G62   Misdirecting user traffic by modifying DNS records is known as *DNS protocol* attack.

G63   The attack where packets are captured by sniffers, information is extracted, and then placed back on the network, is known as *replay* attack.

G64   Tricking a device into thinking that an incorrect IP address is related to a MAC address is known as *ARP poisoning*.

G65   The host hijacked by an attacker to carry out attacks on the victim is known as *zombie*.

G66   Programs written to perform repetitive tasks on the Web are usually known as *bots*.

G67   *Spoofing* facilitates a user/entity to pretend to be someone/something else.

G68   Using forged source addresses is known as *source address spoofing*.

G69   The attack that sends ICMP packets to the broadcast address of a network with spoofed source address to be from the victim's computer is known as *smurf attack*.

G70   Using different keys for encryption for the different directions of a communication channel prevent *reflection attacks*.

G71   A web attack in which a script is embedded in a URL such that when a Web server processes the URL, its reply includes the script within it, is known as *reflected XSS*.

G72   The computers (servers) which are made to send responses to target (victim) clients to the spoofed requests sent by the attacker are known as *intermediaries*.

G73   Packets generated in response to a DoS attack with a forged (spoofed) random source addresses is known as *backscatter traffic*.

G74   In *amplification* attack, multiple replies (responses) are sent by a Web server (intermediary) for each original packet that is sent to it.

G75   In amplification attack the original request is sent by the attacker to the *broadcast* address for some network.

G76   Not allowing directed broadcasts to be routed into a network from outside is good defense against *amplification* attack.

G77   The process of changing email message IDs to look as though they came from someone else is known as *masquerading*.

G78   Making many connection attempts using spoofed source addresses and incomplete handshakes is a sign of *SYN flood* attack.

G79   Excessive traffic on the front-end servers that balance incoming requests among multiple back-end processing servers is a symptom of *SYN flood* attack.

G80   Continuous sending of ACK packets towards a target is known as *ACK flood* attack.

G81   A DDoS attack that floods the target system with a large amount of spoofed UDP traffic to a router's broadcast address is known as *__fraggle attack__*.

G82   Connection requests rerouted to a malicious Web server is a sign of *__DNS hijacking__* attack.

G83   IDS (Intrusion Detection System) logs of incoming malformed packets is a sign of *__ping of death__* attack.

G84   The attack where capturing the traffic from a legitimate session and replaying it with the goal of masquerading as an authenticated user is known as *__replay attack__*.

G85   Technique where bots follow all links on the Web site in a recursive way starting from a given HTTP link, is known as *__spidering__*.

G86   The ICMP echo response packets generated in response to a ping flood using randomly spoofed source addresses is known as *__backscatter__* traffic.

G87   Sending a series of malicious packets to a server is known as *__flooding__*.

G88   An attack that overwhelms Web servers with numerous HTTP requests is known as *__HTTP flood__*.

G89   In reflection attacks, the source addresses of the packets are spoofed with the IP address of the *__victim (target)__*.

G90   Sending a series of DNS requests containing the spoofed source address for the target system is known as *__DNS amplification__* attack.

G91   The attack which uses incorrect handling/checking of program input data to influence the flow of execution of the program is known as *__injection attack__*.

G92   Using the unchecked/incorrectly checked input to construct a malicious command that is subsequently executed by the system with the privileges of the attacked program is known as *command injection* attack.

G93   The attack where the input includes code that is subsequently executed by the target system (victim) is known as *code injection* attack.

G94   The attack which makes use of assignment of global variables to field values in Web forms is known as *PHP remote code injection* attack.

G95   The attack where user supplied input is used to construct a SQL request to retrieve information from a database is known as *SQL injection attack*.

G96   The reachable and exploitable vulnerabilities in a system are known as *attack surfaces*.

G97   The attack which collects an infected user's clicks is known as *clickjacking*.

G98   The attack where a bot starts from a given HTTP link and follows all links on the provided Web site is known as *recursive HTTP flood/attack*.

G99   Recursive HTTP attack is also known as *spidering*.

G100   An already planted malicious script in one of the pages of an insecure web sites installing a malware directly onto the computer of someone who visits the site, is known as *drive-by downloads*.

G101   Simply visiting a Web site containing malicious script via a vulnerable browser (client) can result in a *drive-by download* attack.

G102   Password guessing attack is carried out at the *application* layer of the network.

G103   SYN flood attacks are carried out at the *transport* layer of the network.

G104 Scans for vulnerable ports are carried out at the *__transport__* layer.

G105 Attacks using spoofed IP addresses are carried out at the *__network__* layer.

G106 Attacks using illegal IP header values are carried out at the *__network__* layer.

G107 An attacker sending a flood of malformed or malicious pings to a computer is known as *__ping of death (PoD)__* attack.

G108 Reassembly of malformed packet fragments resulting in an oversized packet, leading to buffer overflow is known as *__ping of death (PoD)__* attack.

G109 Sending a stream of ICMP Echo Request (ping) packets without waiting for replies is known as *__ICMP flood__* attack.

G110 A DoS / DDoS attack that floods a target with user datagram protocol (UDP) packets is known as *__UDP flood attack__*.

G111 The attack where actual database commands are inserted in place of valid input, which are run by the application is known as *__SQL injection__*.

G112 The denial of service (DoS) attack on the Web is an attack on the *__availability__* aspect of the CIA triad.

G113 In a Distributed Denial of Service (DDoS) attack with N Zombies, each with a connection bandwidth of W bps (bits/sec), and the target machine with a connection bandwidth of X bps, the required condition for the attack to succeed is *__$NW > X$__*

G114 In the *__ciphertext only__* attack, the encryption algorithm and ciphertext are known to the cryptanalyst.

G115 In the *__known plaintext only__* attack, the encryption algorithm, ciphertext, and one or more plaintext-ciphertext pairs are known to the cryptanalyst.

G116   Several commonly used file formats begin with well-known patterns (headers) and could therefore be prone to **_known plaintext_** attack.

G117   The attack where sender is made to generate ciphertext for a specific plaintext (chosen by the attacker) is known as **_chosen plaintext_** attack.

G118   The attack used for tricking users to disclose their username and passwords through fake pages is known as **_phishing_**.

G119   Unsolicited Bulk E-mails are called **_spam_** emails.

G120   Rejection of external packets to broadcast address helps prevent **_smurf_** attack.

G121   Configuring the routers to not forward packets directed to broadcast addresses helps prevent **_smurf_** attack.

G122   Termination of the Internet connection by sending a forged TCP reset packet is known as **_TCP reset attack_**.

G123   In a(n) **_Cross-Site Scripting (XSS)_** attack an attacker is able to inject client-side scripts into Web pages.

G124   The attack where a client repeatedly sends SYN (synchronization) packets to every port on a server (usually) using fake IP addresses is known as **_SYN flood_** attack.

G125   *Half-open* attack is another name for **_SYN flood_** attack.

G126   Sending a series of connection requests (SYN packets) before the prior connections can time out is indication of **_SYN flood_** attack.

G127   The attacker sending TCP connection requests faster than the target (victim) machine can process is known as the **_SYN flood_** attack.

G128   In SYN flood attack, the attacker sends a series of **_SYN_** packets to the victim machine, but does not send the **_ACK_** packets to the victim, in response to the victim's **_SYN+ACK_** packets.

G129   Host *A* sending TCP connection requests to host *B*, but not responding to *B*'s messages to complete the connection is indicative of **_SYN flood_** attack.

G130   Attack in which a rogue DHCP server sends forged DHCP responses to devices in a network is known as **_DHCP Spoofing_**.

G131   An effective method to shield networks from unauthenticated DHCP clients is via the use of **_DHCP snooping_** on network switches.

G132   Ensuring that DHCP servers assign IP addresses to only selected systems identified by their MAC addresses is known as **_DHCP snooping_**.

G133   **_DHCP snooping_** prevents unauthorized (rogue) DHCP servers from offering IP addresses to DHCP clients.

G134   Timing attacks in public-key cryptography systems involve extensive analysis of **_decryption_** times in order to determine private key.

G135   An attacker taking control of a session between the server and a client is known as **_TCP/IP hijacking_**.

G136   Changing the mapping of domain name to IP address in DNS server or DNS cache is known as **_DNS poisoning_**.

G137   Redirecting traffic intended for a (genuine) Web site to some other (rogue) site is achieved by changing the **_IP record (address)_** for that Web site in **_DNS server (or in DNS cache)_**.

G138   The attack which redirects traffic intended for a (genuine) Web site to some other (rogue) site is known as **_DNS spoofing (or DNS poisoning)_**.

G139   An attack that redirects victims to a bogus website, even after correctly inputting the intended site is known as **_pharming_**.

G140   Email attack that is targeted toward a specific user is known as **_spear phishing_**.

G141　Attack using a fake caller-ID posing as a trusted organization attempting to get sensitive information via the phone is known as *vishing* (voice phishing).

G142　Attacks that use phishing methods through text messaging are known as *smishing* (SMS phishing).

G143　Type of spam targeting users of instant messaging (IM) services is known as *spim*.

G144　False information (propaganda) about an attack which is not existent is known as *hoax*.

G145　Smurfing attack is also known as *Ping flooding* or *ICMP storm*.

G146　Process used to identify weaknesses of cryptosystems by locating patterns in the ciphertext is known as *frequency analysis*.

G147　The worst-case time (trying all key possibilities) required to break a key of length L bits, while processing K keys per second, is $2^L / K$ seconds.

G148　While processing K keys per second, the length L of a key that can be broken in a given time T (in the worst-case) is $\log_2 (K \cdot T)$ bits.

G149　Preinstalled public keys of the root CAs in the client (PC/laptop) browsers defends the root-level verification against *man-in-the-middle* attack.

G150　Use of random delays or blinding computations are countermeasures to thwart *timing* attacks.

G151　A bad web site sending browser request to a good web site, using credentials of an innocent victim is known as *cross-site request forgery (CSRF)*.

G152　The cryptanalysis technique which attempt to deduce information from traffic patterns is known as *traffic analysis*.

G153　The botnet (network of bots) is remotely controlled by the hacker (*bot herder*) usually through the *Internet Relay Chat (IRC)* protocol.

G154   A technique used to thwart dictionary attacks on passwords is known as *__salting__*.

G155   Enforcing re-authentication of users before allowing transactions to occur, mitigates *__session hijacking__*.

G156   The process wherein the response from the victim system to an attacker is deliberately delayed to the point of timing out the connection is known as *__tarpit__*.

G157   Placing code within a web page that redirects the client's browser to attack another site upon opening the web page in client's browser is known as *__cross-file scripting (XSS)__*.

G158   Insertion of bits in data stream with the purpose of thwarting traffic analysis is known as *__traffic padding__*.

H. Network Security

H1   The **_IPSec_** is security added between the TCP and IP layers.

H2   The security mechanism most commonly used with Hypertext Transfer Protocol (HTTP) is **_Secure Sockets Layer (SSL) / Transport Layer Security (TLS)_**.

H3   Secure Sockets Layer (SSL) has now been replaced by **_Transport Layer Security (TLS)_**.

H4   The TLS handshake uses **_public key_** encryption to establish a shared key between the two computers.

H5   The protocol which handles the echo request/reply messages for the ping command is the **_ICMP_**.

H6   The number of encryption devices required in the link encryption with N links between a pair of hosts is **$2N$**.

H7   The number of encryption devices required in the end-to-end encryption with N links between a pair of hosts is **2**.

H8   A packet going over N links using link encryption is encrypted/decrypted **$2N$** times.

H9   The security protocol used for tunneling in a VPN is **_IPSec_**.

H10   A free and open-source software which facilitates anonymous communication is **_Tor (The onion router)_**.

H11   In Tor (The onion router) the only IP address visible to the destination website is that of the **_final node (exit node)_**.

H12   All the traffic arriving at the destination node via a Tor network will have the source address of the **_Tor exit_** node.

H13   The protocol which provides the essential routing function of all packets is the **_Internet protocol (IP)_**.

H14   The protocol which provides reliable processes to process communication is the *transmission control protocol (TCP)*.

H15   The protocol which transmits control messages between networked devices is the *Internet control message protocol (ICMP)*.

H16   Secure HTTP functions at the *application* layer.

H17   For gateway-to-gateway communications, IPSec runs mainly in *tunnel* mode.

H18   For host-to-host communications, IPSec runs mainly in *transport* mode.

H19   IPSec encrypts only the packet payload in *transport* mode of VPN.

H20   IPSec encrypts both the packet payload and header in *tunnel* mode.

H21   In the *tunnel* mode of VPN, both header and body of messages are encrypted.

H22   In the *transport* mode of VPN only the payload is encrypted.

H23   In the *transport* mode of VPN, two remote hosts on secure (private) networks can directly establish a secure (logical) link going via a public network (Internet).

H24   In the *transport* mode of VPN, individual hosts on secure (private) networks perform encryption of messages.

H25   In the *tunneling* mode of VPN, designated server performs encryption of packets going from the secure private network to the public network (Internet).

H26   The *ping* command makes use of the *ICMP* protocol.

H27   The command used to determine if a host is active on a network is *ping*.

H28   In SSL, the initial vector (IV) is sent during **_SSL handshake_**.

H29   SSL (Secure Sockets Layer) works between **_application_** and **_transport_** (of TCP/IP protocol) layers.

H30   Agreement on the cipher schemes to be employed during the SSL session is done during **_SSL handshake_**.

H31   The security services provided by SSL record protocol for messages are **_confidentiality_** and **_integrity_**.

H32   Encapsulating security payload (ESP) is a protocol used in **_IPSec_**.

H33   Port scan to determine if a TCP port is open, sends out **_TCP SYN segment_**.

H34   An application layer protocol that facilitates managing and monitoring the network devices is **_simple network management protocol (SNMP)_**.

H35   Remote users on private networks can communicate securely using intermediary insecure public network (ex. Internet) using **_Virtual Private Network (VPN)_**.

H36   The two types of VPNs are **_remote access_** VPNs and **_site-to-site (router-to-router)_** VPNs.

H37   Site-to-site VPNs are also known as **_router-to-router_** VPNs.

H38   Individual users can connect to private networks at home and access resources remotely using **_remote access_** VPNs.

H39   A remote-access VPN typically depends on either **_Secure Sockets Layer (SSL)_** or **_IP Security (IPsec)_** for secure connection over public network (Internet).

H40   Mapping of host/site names to numeric IP addresses is done by **_Domain Name System/Server (DNS)_**.

H41   Reverse name lookup means fetching **_the symbolic hostname_** associated with a **_numeric IP address_**.

H42   The detection of hosts or devices in a network is known as *network enumeration*.

H43   Ping sweep is also known as *ICMP* sweep.

H44   Technique that facilitates mapping of IP address to live hosts is known as *ICMP sweep*.

H45   *Wireshark* is a popular standardized network protocol analysis tool that allows in-depth check and analysis of packets from different protocols.

H46   A technique used by penetration testers to compromise any system within a network for targeting other systems is known as *pivoting*.

H47   Checking for live systems, open ports and identification of services running on the systems are done using *ICMP scanning*.

H48   The network scanning technique used for determining which range of IP addresses map to live/running hosts is known as *ping sweep*.

H49   The ping sweep consists of *ICMP ECHO* requests.

H50   SSL uses *MAC (Message Authentication Code)* for authenticating messages.

H51   IPSec (Secure Internet Protocol) makes use of *three* different protocols for securing data at the network level.

H52   The three different protocols used by IPSec are *Encapsulating Secure Payload (ESP)*, *Authentication Header (AH)*, and *Internet Key Exchange (IKE)*.

H53   The protocol used for starting, preserving and terminating any real time sessions over the internet is the *session initiation protocol (SIP)*.

H54   Ensuring that the traffic originating from a given domain (outbound traffic) have valid source addresses is known as *egress* filtering.

H55 Blocking all outgoing packets with source IP addresses which are outside the range assigned to the network, is known as *egress filtering*.

H56 Blocking all incoming packets having source IP addresses assigned to computers inside the network, is known as *ingress filtering*.

H57 The security properties provided by TLS are *confidentiality*, *integrity*, and *(one-way) authentication*.

H58 In TLS, messages are encrypted using *session keys*.

H59 In TLS, message integrity is provided by the use of *message authentication code (MAC)*.

H60 In TLS, the servers authenticate themselves to the clients by the use of *signed certificates*.

H61 The SSL (TLS) takes unencrypted data from the *application* layer, encrypts it and then passes it to the *transport* layer.

H62 *IPSec* provides security to data passing from transport layer (TCP) to network layer (IP).

H63 The process where two entities first exchange control packets before sending data to each other is called *handshaking*.

H64 The process of gathering IP addresses of machines on the network, the operating systems on the machines, is known as *network mapping*.

H65 The cryptographic parameters used between two computers using SSL or TLS are negotiated/exchanges using a series of steps known as *handshaking*.

H66 The three cryptographic protections provided by SSL and TLS are *confidentiality*, *authentication*, and *message integrity*.

H67 In IPSec, the secret key together with a set of cryptographic parameters is known as *security association (SA)*.

H68   In IPSec, the attribute which specifies whether the data packet is protected by confidentiality or message integrity or both is known as *protocol* attribute.

H69   In IPSec, the attribute which specifies how much of the data packet is protected is known as *mode* attribute.

H70   The two mode attributes (choices) of IPSec are *tunnel* and *transport*.

H71   Tunnel mode IPSec is commonly used in *site-to-site* VPN.

H72   Transport mode IPSec is commonly used in *remote-access* VPN.

H73   In *transport* mode, IPsec header is inserted into the IP packet.

H74   In *tunnel* mode, entire IP packet is encrypted and becomes a payload of a new IP packet.

H75   The functionalities provided by IPsec are *authentication*, *encryption*, and *key exchange*.

H76   The combined authentication/encryption function of IPSec is provided by *Encapsulating Security Payload (ESP)*.

H77   In a VPN, prevention of unauthorized users from penetrating the virtual private network is done using *authentication*.

H78   In a VPN, prevention unauthorized users from reading messages sent over the virtual private network is done using *encryption*.

H79   In a VPN (Virtual Private Network), the mechanism of sending a packet through a public network between private networks is known as *tunneling*.

H80   *IPSec* provides security at the *network* layer.

H81   *TLS* provides security at the *transport* layer.

H82   *SSL* (Secure Socket Layer) provides security at the *transport* layer.

H83   *PGP* provides security at the ***application*** layer.

H84   The number of times the body of the packet is encrypted + decrypted when sent from a host A to a host B via N links using end-to-end encryption is **$2N$**.
[2 times per link]

H85   A packet with the correct checksum, but failing the integrity check is rejected by the ***SSL*** at the receiver.

H86   Given M hosts communicating over a network path with N links, the number of encryption devices required in the combined link and end-to-end encryption is **$2N + M$**
[2 devices/link and 1 for each host]

H87   The packets of a message sent from a host A to a host B over N links using link encryption is encrypted **N** times.
[1 encryption for every link]

H88   The packets of a message sent from a host A to a host B over N links using combined end-to-end and link encryption is encrypted **$N + 1$** times.
[1 encryption for every link, and 1 encryption at the sender]

H89   The number of times a message (packet) is encrypted going from host A to a host B via N links with end-to-end encryption is **2**.

H90   The number of times the header of packet is encrypted going from host A to a host B via N links with link encryption is **N**.

H91   Given that the header of a packet is encrypted 18 times going from host A to a host B using link encryption, the number of intermediary links between A and B, is **18**.

H92   Given that a packet (header/body) going from host A to a host B using combined link and end-to-end encryption is subjected to a total of 18 encryptions/decryptions, the number of intermediary links between A and B, is **8**.

H93   Multiple systems can share a single IP address using a service known as ***Network Address Translation (NAT)***.

H94   A standard protocol for transmitting and receiving files from client to server through a network is the ***File Transfer Protocol (FTP)***.

H95   A port number is always associated with ***IP address*** of the host and the ***communication protocol***.

H96   The port number of File Transfer Protocol (FTP) for data transfer is **20**.

H97   The port number of File Transfer Protocol (FTP) is for control signals is **21**.

H98   The port number of Secure Shell (SSH) which is used for secure login is **22**.

H99   The port number of Telnet which is used for remote login service is **23**.

H100   The port number of Simple Mail Transfer Protocol (SMTP) E-mail routing is **25**.

H101   The port number of Domain Name System (DNS) service is **53**.

H102   The port number of Dynamic Host Configuration Protocol (DHCP) is **67, 68**.

H103   The port number of Hypertext Transfer Protocol (HTTP) is **80**.

H104   The Port number of Kerberos service is **88**.

H105   The port number of Post Office Protocol (POP3) is **110**.

H106   The port number of Network News Transfer Protocol (NNTP) is **119**.

H107   The port number of Network Time Protocol (NTP) is **123**.

H108   The port number of Internet Message Access Protocol (IMAP) is **143**.

H109   The port number(s) of Simple Network Management Protocol (SNMP) is (are) **161, 162**.

H110   The port number of Internet Relay Chat (IRC) is **194**.

H111   The port number of HTTPS (HTTP Secure – HTTP over TLS/SSL) is **443**.

H112   Bridges work at the ***data link*** layer.

H113   Routers work at the ***network*** layer.

H114   The host (or device or software) that connects two different environments is known as ***gateway***.

H115   ICMP works at the ***network*** layer.

H116   ***Network Address Translation (NAT)*** enables a LAN to use one set of IP addresses for internal traffic and another set of addresses for external traffic.

H117   A signaling protocol widely used for VoIP communications sessions is the ***Session Initiation Protocol (SIP).***

H118   Ensuring that valid source addresses are used in all packets can be (fairly) easily done at the ***Internet Service Provider (ISP)***.

H119   TCP and UDP port scanning is carried out at the ***transport*** layer.

H120   ICMP scanning is carried out at the ***network*** layer.

H121   FTPS (FTP Secure) is an extension of the file transfer protocol (FTP) that adds security via the use of ***Transport Layer Security (TLS)***.

H122   The protocol used for monitoring the health of network equipment, computers, and devices is the ***Simple Network Management Protocol (SNMP)***.

H123   IP protocol is a connectionless protocol that deals with the ***addressing*** and ***routing*** of packets.

H124   The protocol which assigns dynamic IP addresses to hosts (on power-up) is ***Dynamic Host Configuration Protocol (DHCP)***.

H125   The routing where a packet goes through a network on a predetermined path is known as **_source routing_**.

H126   **_Domain Name System Security Extensions (DNSSEC)_** is a set of extensions to DNS which provides cryptographic authentication of DNS data to DNS clients.

H127   The SSL **_handshake_** protocol is layered on top of SSL **_record_** protocol.

H128   The **_SYN_** and **_ACK_** segments are needed to begin a TCP connection.

H129   TLS uses **_public-key_** cryptography for authenticating the identity of the communicating parties.

H130   Upon receiving a SYN packet, a port on a remote host that is open for incoming connection requests, will respond with a **_SYN+ACK_** packet.

H131   Upon receiving a SYN packet, a port on a remote host that is closed for incoming connection requests, will respond with a(n) **_RST_** packet.

H132   Record in DNS containing the Internet email route is called **_mail exchange (MX)_** record.

H133   The protocol which does the translation of IP address to MAC (media access control) address is the **_Address Resolution Protocol (ARP)_**.

H134   ARP (Address Resolution Protocol) poisoning affects the translation of **_IP address_** to **_MAC address_**.

H135   The unique **48** bit identifier assigned to a network card (network interface controller-NIC) is called **_MAC address_**.

H136   The most common way of providing secure connection to remote users over an insecure network (ex. Internet) is via **_Virtual Private Network (VPN)_**.

H137   Encapsulating Security Payload (ESP) part of the IPSec protocol suite, is primarily designed to provide *confidentiality*.

H138   The standards-based version of Secure Sockets Layer (SSL) version 3 is known as *Transport Layer Security (TLS)*.

H139   Security controls at the *transport* layer can be used to protect the data in a single communication session between two hosts.

H140   Address Resolution Protocol (ARP) reply contains the correct mapping between *Media Access Control (MAC)* and *Internet Protocol (IP)* addresses.

H141   An intermediate LAN that is between two screening routers (or firewalls) of a network is known as *demilitarized zone (DMZ)*.

H142   The network of essential servers (ex. Web server, email server) placed between a private (trusted) network and the Internet (public network), is known as *demilitarized zone (DMZ)*.

H143   Encapsulating packets of an internal (private) network protocol into a packet of an external network protocol (typically the Internet) and transmitting is known as *tunneling*.

H144   The IPSec protocol responsible for creation and maintenance of security associations between communicating devices is the *Internet SecurityAssociation And Key Management Protocol (ISAKMP)*.

H145   The authentication header (AH) of IPSec provides *integrity* and *authentication* of messages.

H146   The encapsulating security protection (ESP) of IPSec provides *confidentiality*, *integrity*, and *authentication* of messages.

H147   The port that should be blocked when it has been determined that an intruder has been using Telnet for unauthorized access is **23**.

H148   The port(s) that should be blocked when it has been determined that an intruder has been using SNMP for unauthorized access is/are **161, 162**.

H149   An established connection without specifying a username or password is known as ***null session***.

H150   Information about which key is being used with a packet (key-to-packet mapping) is known as ***security association***.

H151   The protocol used for network diagnostics and performance is ***ICMP***.

H152   The maximum size of a block transported by SSL record protocol is $2^{14} = 16,384$ ***bytes***.

H153   A software utility that scans a single machine or a range of IP addresses checking for a response on service connections is known as ***port scanner***.

H154   ***Vulnerability scanner*** is a software utility that scans a range of IP addresses checking for known weaknesses in software configuration and accessible services.

H155   A software utility that is used to analyze network communications is known as ***protocol analyzer***.

H156   A software utility that compiles a list of all systems, devices, and network hardware present within a network segment is known as ***network mapper***.

H157   ***Vulnerability scanner*** is an assessment tool for checking particular versions and patch levels of a service.

H158   ***Network mapper*** is an assessment tool that reports information used to identify single points of failure.

H159   Protocol analyzer is also often referred to as ***packet sniffer***.

H160   Routing where the sender of a packet can partially or completely specify the route the packet takes through the network is known as ***source routing***.

H161   The most commonly used message authentication code (MAC) used in IPSec is ***HMAC (Hash-based Message Authentication Code)***.

H162   The technical controls that track activity within a network, on a network device, or on a computer are known as ___*auditing tools*___.

H163   The routing tables at the routers are based on ___*IP*___ addresses.

H164   The protocol for accessing and maintaining distributed directory information services in a network using Internet Protocol (IP) is the ___*Lightweight Directory Access Protocol (LDAP)*___.

H165   Message security being maintained, despite being sent over insecure channel, is known as ___*object security*___.

H166   Under channel security, message security relies on protocols below the ___*application*___ layer to handle the encryption.

H167   The process of trying to list all servers in a network is known as ___*enumeration*___.

I. Web Security and Application Security

I1   **_S/MIME_** is another widely used Email security system other than PGP.

I2   The private–public key pairs of a user in PGP are stored in the **_private_** key ring.

I3   To make it compatible with many Email systems, PGP performs **_Radix-64 conversion_**.

I4   The number of key rings maintained by PGP is **2**.

I5   The session key in PGP is encrypted using the recipient's **_public_** key.

I6   Typically the **_user's email address_** is used as the user ID in the private key ring of PGP.

I7   The number of bits used to index the Radix-64 conversion table of PGP is **6**.

I8   The portion of the World Wide Web that a common (popular) search engine cannot search is known as the **_deep Web_ (or _hidden Web_)**.

I9   The portion of the Web that is indexed by common (popular) search engine(s) is known as **_surface web_**.

I10   In the first instance, a cookie is sent from a **_Web server_** to a **_client Web browser_**.

I11   The portion of the Web that is accessible only via onion routing is known as **_the dark Web_**.

I12   The cookie that exists only in temporary memory while the user navigates the website is known as **_session cookie / transient cookie / non-persistent cookie_**.

I13   The cookie that still exists even after a user has finished navigation of the Web site is known as **_persistent cookie_**.

I14   A cookie that can only be transmitted over an encrypted connection (https) is known as ***secure cookie***.

I15   One way of not revealing the IP address of a computer (client) to any Web server is to use a(n) ***anonymous proxy server*** that sits between the client and the Internet.

I16   Cookies that are sent only over HTTPS connection are known as ***secure-cookies***.

I17   A cookie is just a data file containing the 'state' of interaction between the ***browser* (client)** and ***the server***.

I18   A cookie that is stored only in memory but not in a file is known as a ***session cookie***.

I19   Software installed on a system that is designed to intercept all traffic between the local web browser and the web server is known as ***web proxy***.

I20   Secure key exchange between the Web server and Web browser id provided by ***secure socket layer (SSL)***.

I21   The scheme used for message encryption in current versions of S/MIME is ***AES***.

I22   In S/MIME, the ElGamal public key scheme (by default) is used to encrypt ***the session key***.

I23   The default algorithms used for signing S/MIME messages are the ***Digital Signature Standard (DSS)*** and the ***Secure Hash Algorithm (SHA-1)***.

I24   The SET (Secure Electronic Transaction) provides security at the ***application*** layer of the network.

I25   In SET, the session key K_S used to encrypt the payment information is itself encrypted using the ***public key of the bank***.

I26   The ***cross-site scripting*** vulnerability can be mitigated by preventing the use of HTML tags.

I27   In the e-commerce transactions between a user and business using only one-way authentication, *the user laptop (client/browser)* needs to authenticate *the business Website (server)*.

I28   Pretty Good Privacy (PGP) is used in *email* application.

I29   Cookies that are created by domains other than the one a user is visiting directly, are known as *third-party cookies*.

I30   Certificates commonly used in Web applications for secure client-server communication are *SSL certificates*.

I31   The *session (or temporary)* cookies are deleted when the browser is exited.

I32   A single machine serving many web sites (by having many hostnames corresponding to a single IP address) is known as *virtual hosting*.

I33   A mail server can look up the IP of an incoming mail connection and reject it if it is listed in the *DNS-based blacklist*.

I34   The return addresses in the headers of all packets leaving a private network (intranet) using a proxy server are changed to the address of the *proxy server*.

I35   In onion routing, all servers (except the origin and destination) via which packets are sent are *proxy servers*.

I36   Input validation is done at the client before it is sent to the server to process is known as *client-side validation*.

I37   Both HTTP and HTTPS content downloaded to browser while displaying in the same page is known as *mixed content*.

I38   An XML-based language for the exchange of security information among online business partners is *security assertion markup language (SAML)*.

I39   In encrypted email systems, raw 8-bit binary stream is converted to a stream of printable ASCII characters using *radix 64 conversion*.

I40   Validation of values received by a server application to be within permissible limits, before processing them, is known as ***parameter validation***.

I41   The technology that allows web developers to reuse content by inserting the same content into multiple web documents is known as ***server side includes (SSI)***.

I42   A decoy system that is designed to lure a potential attacker away from a critical system is known as ***honey pot***.

I43   A ***tarpit*** delivers suspected SPAM messages with more delays.

I44   In PGP, the integrity of the message is ensured by the use of ***digital signature***.

I45   While using an anonymizing proxy server, the traffic between a user and the proxy will be encrypted by using ***SSL***.

I46   Rejection of email from specific IP addresses is facilitated by ***DNS blacklisting***.

J. Firewalls and Intrusion Detection

J1   The simplest among the types of firewalls is the ***packet-filtering*** firewall.

J2   Firewall installed on a single computer to prevent intrusion is known as ***host-based*** firewall.

J3   Packet filtering firewalls are implemented in the ***network*** layer.

J4   The table containing rules for firewall system to provide/deny entry to packets is called ***access control list (ACL)***.

J5   Packet filtering firewalls determine the validity of every packet by checking against the rules defined in the ***access control list (ACL)***.

J6   A packet filtering firewall makes decision about allowing or dropping a packet based on the rules defined in the ***access control list (ACL)***.

J7   A computer (system) which acts as a relay for application-level traffic between two remote hosts is known as ***application level gateway***.

J8   Stateful Multilayer Inspection firewalls are a combination of (other three types of) ***packet filtering***, ***circuit level***, and ***application-level gateway*** firewalls.

J9   The firewall with built in algorithms and complex security modes is the ***stateful multilayer inspection*** firewall.

J10   The firewall incorporating multiple characteristics of different firewalls is the ***stateful multilayer inspection*** firewall.

J11   Software running on a single host that restricts incoming and outgoing network activity for that host only is known as ***host-based*** firewall.

J12   A device deployed between networks to restrict the types of traffic that can pass from one network to another is known as ***network firewall***.

J13   The default *deny* policy of a firewall is comparatively more restrictive.

J14   Firewalls that use the contents of packets together with information about other packets and connections are known as *stateful* firewalls.

J15   Spoofed IP packets can be prevented from leaving a network by packet filter firewall by examining the *IP source address* of the packet.

J16   The first firewall faced by traffic coming from the Internet to an internal (protected) network is known as *external firewall*.

J17   The firewall closest to the internal network of hosts is known as *internal firewall*.

J18   A firewall placed at the perimeter of the network as the sole link between the network and the outside world is known as *bastion host*.

J19   The rule which protects the firewall from attacks is known as *stealth* rule.

J20   Allowing all connections *except* explicitly specified connections is known as *blacklisting*.

J21   Disallowing all connections *except* explicitly specified connections is known as *whitelisting*.

J22   A *stateless* firewall analyzes packets independently, without regard to other packets.

J23   Statistical filtering is also known as *Bayesian filtering*.

J24   *Application level gateway* firewalls protect the network for specific application layer protocol.

J25   The filtering rules of packet filters are set by *the network administrator*.

J26   The primary defenses against network mapping are *firewalls* and *intrusion detection systems*.

J27   Servers that act as intermediaries between the public network and private servers are known as *application-level gateways*.

J28   The firewall which in addition to examining each packet, also uses data derived from several previous packets is known as *stateful packet inspection (SPI)* firewall.

J29   Application-level gateways are also known as *proxies*.

J30   The firewall where each incoming packet is examined, and allowing only the ones matching the set of criteria is called *packet-filtering* firewall.

J31   Application level gateway is also known as *application proxy* - firewall.

J32   In a *stateless* firewall the criteria for deciding to pass or discard the packet are (1) *information in the packet header* and (2) the *firewall's rules*.

J33   Routers acting as firewalls process packets at the *transport* layer.

J34   A *network-based IDS* monitors traffic at selected points on a network.

J35   A network-based IDS primarily performs *packet sniffing* and *network traffic analysis* to identify suspicious activity.

J36   Part of the IDS that is responsible for collecting data is known as *sensor*.

J37   Part of the IDS that receives input from one or more sensors and determines if an intrusion has occurred is known as *analyzer*.

J38   A sensor of an IDS through which the actual traffic passes is known as *inline sensor*.

J39   In the context of IDS, authorized users identified as intruders are known as *false positives (false alarms)*.

J40 In the context of IDS, intruders not identified as intruders are known as *false negatives*.

J41 In the context of IDS, the ratio of detected attacks to total attacks is known as *detection rate*.

J42 The *heuristic (anomaly based)* IDS (Intrusion Detection System) looks for deviations from the model of accepted behavior.

J43 Nonintrusive activities misclassified as attacks are known as *false positives*.

J44 Malicious activities which fail to be identified and pass through as genuine activities are known as *false negatives*.

J45 The *statistical/anomaly-based* intrusion detection system monitors user and network behavior.

J46 Intrusion Prevention System (IPS) that monitors the characteristics and the events occurring within a single host is known as *host-based IPS*.

J47 *Rule-based* intrusion detection is only effective in detecting known attacks.

J48 *Anomaly-detection* intrusion detection is effective in detecting novel (previously unknown) attacks.

J49 Monitoring the activities and the events within a single host for suspicious activities is done by *host-based* IDS.

J50 Defining and using a set of rules or attack patterns to decide if a given behavior is that of an intruder in done in *signature* detection.

IOIOIOIOIOIOIOIOIOIOIOIOIOIOIOIOIOIOIOIOIOIOIOIOIOIOIOIOIOIOI

Books on Computer Security

- W. Stallings and L. Brown. *Computer Security Principles and Practice* (3rd Edition). Pearson 2015. ISBN 9780133773927.

- C.P. Pfleeger, S.L. Pfleeger, and J. Margulies. *Security in Computing* (5th Edition). Prentice–Hall, 2016. ISBN: 9780134085043.

- A.D. Rubin. *White-Hat Security Arsenal*. Addison-Wesley, 2001. ISBN: 0201711141.

- C. Easttom. *Computer Security Fundamentals* (4th Edition). Pearson, 2020. ISBN: 9780135774779.

- M.G. Solomon and M. Chapple. *Information Security Illuminated*. Jones and Bartlett, 2008. ISBN: 9780763726775.

- M. Bishop. *Computer Security* (2nd Edition). Addison-Wesley, 2018. ISBN: 9780321712332.

- M. Bishop. *Introduction to Computer Security*. Addison-Wesley, 2005. ISBN: 0321247442.

- R. J. Anderson. *Security Engineering: A Guide to Building Dependable Distributed Systems* (2nd Edition). Wiley, 2008. ISBN: 9780470068526.

- N. Ferguson, B. Schneier, and T. Kohno. *Cryptography Engineering – Design Principles and Practical Applications*. Wiley, 2010. ISBN: 9780470474242.

- B. Schneier. *Applied Cryptography – Protocols, Algorithms, and Source Code in C*. Wiley, 1996. ISBN 9781119096726.

Other Related Quiz Books

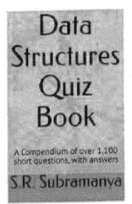

This is a quick assessment book / quiz book. It has a vast collection of over 1,100 questions, with answers on Data Structures. Questions have a wide range of difficulty levels and are designed to test a thorough understanding of the topical material. The coverage includes elementary and advanced data structures – Arrays (single/multidimensional); Linked lists (singly–linked, doubly–linked, circular); Stacks; Queues; Heaps; Hash tables; Binary trees; Binary search trees; Balanced trees (AVL trees, Red–Black trees, B–trees/B+ trees); Graphs.

This is a quick assessment book / quiz book. It has a vast collection of over 1,000 questions, with answers on Algorithms. The book covers questions on standard (classical) algorithm design techniques; sorting and searching; graph traversals; minimum spanning trees; shortest path problems; maximum flow problems; elementary concepts in P and NP Classes. It also covers a few specialized areas – string processing; polynomial operations; numerical & matrix computations; computational geometry & computer graphics

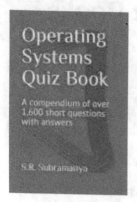

This is a quick assessment book / quiz book. It has a wide variety of over 1,600 questions, with answers on Operating Systems. The questions have a wide range of difficulty levels and are designed to test a thorough understanding of the topical material. The book covers questions on the operating systems structures, fundamentals of processes and threads, CPU scheduling, process synchronization, deadlocks, memory management, I/O subsystem, and mass storage (disk) structures.

This is a quick assessment book / quiz book. It has wide variety of ~1,400 questions on Programming Languages and Compilers. It covers questions on: Bindings and Scopes, Data types, Expressions and Assignment statements, Subprograms and Parameter passing mechanisms, Abstract Data Types, Object- Oriented constructs, and Exception handling. The topics related to Compilers include programming language syntax and semantics, lexical analysis, parsing, and different parsing techniques.

This is a quick assessment book / quiz book. It has a vast collection of over 1,200 short questions, with answers and programs, on Java programming language. The topical coverage includes data types, control structures, arrays, classes, objects, and methods, inheritance and polymorphism, exception handling, and stream and text I/O

This is a quick assessment book / quiz book. It has a vast collection of over 1,000 short questions, with answers and programs, on C++ programming language. The topical coverage includes data types, control structures, arrays, pointers and reference, classes and objects, inheritance and polymorphism, exception handling, and stream and text I/O.

This is a quick assessment book / quiz book. It has a vast collection of over 1,100 short questions, with answers and programs, on C programming language. It covers all the major topics of C programming – data types, operators, expressions, control structures, pointers, arrays, structures, unions, enumerated types, functions, dynamic storage management, I/O and Library functions.

This is a quick assessment book / quiz book. It has a vast collection of over 1,500 short questions, with answers. It covers all the major topics in a typical first course in Computer Networks. The coverage includes, the various layers of the Internet (TCP/IP) protocol stack (going from the actual transmission of signals to the applications that users use) – physical layer, data link layer, network layer, transport layer, and application layer, network security, and Web security.

This is a self–assessment / quiz /exercise book. It has a vast collection of over 1,200 questions, with solutions, in Discrete Mathematics. Questions have a wide range of difficulty levels and are designed to test a thorough understanding of the topical material. The topical coverage includes: Logic and Proof methods, Sets, Functions, Relations, Properties of integers, Sequences, Induction and Recursion, Basic and advanced counting methods, Discrete probability, Graph theory, Modeling computation, and Boolean algebra.

www.ingramcontent.com/pod-product-compliance
Lightning Source LLC
LaVergne TN
LVHW051436050326
832903LV00030BD/3112